'This is a dynamic read! We ~~~~~~ ~~~~
read this book, I hadn't giv ~~~~~~
during and after the great f ~~~~~~
the scene alive, with helpfu ~~~~~~
really like to have lived during those turbulent ~~~~
does the whole experience speak to us today? A truly original look
at the Noah's ark story, from the women's perspective. Relevant,
timely and deeply thought-provoking.'
Sheila Jacobs, editor and CBC award-winning author

'As in the days of Noah... Jocelyn-Anne Harvey has written an
insightful and timely book drawing striking parallels between our
present reality with what Noah and the women of his family might
have experienced aboard the Ark. *Not Knowing but Still Going* offers
a fresh perspective on how to navigate "unchartered waters" and
adjust to new "norms" – while reminding us of "the rainbow of
His promise" to face the days ahead.'
Darla Milne, author of Second Chance

'*Not Knowing but Still Going* provokes the reader to view life on the
ark through the eyes of the four women on board. An easy read,
and biblically sound, it has thought-provoking questions at the end
of each chapter which would be ideal for women's group Bible
study.'
*Karen Johnson, Ministry Coordinator at Creation Ministries International
(UK)*

'Although we find ourselves living in unprecedented times, we
have been prepared, because the Lord told us it would be like the
days of Noah. Jocelyn-Anne does an amazing job of bringing to
life the challenges that Noah and his family must have experienced
walking into the unknown, just like we are doing now. The
emotional and spiritual difficulties and how we can move forward
in victory, looking unto Jesus for strength and peace in the midst
of the storm. Being confident of God's goodness and sovereignty
through it all.'
Jeff Cuozzo, Pastor Calvary Bath, UK & Europe Coordinator Behold Israel

NOT KNOWING
but Still Going

Jocelyn-Anne Harvey

instant
apostle

First published in Great Britain in 2021

Instant Apostle
104 The Drive
Rickmansworth
Herts
WD3 4DU

Anglicised, NIV® Copyright © 1979, 1984, 2011 by Biblica, Inc.®
Used by permission. All rights reserved worldwide.

Ark illustration: Penelope Harvey

Author photograph: Stephanie Hutchings

Every effort has been made to seek permission to use copyright
material reproduced in this book. The publisher apologises for
those cases where permission might not have been sought and,
if notified, will formally seek permission at the earliest
opportunity.

The views and opinions expressed in this work are those of the
author and do not necessarily reflect the views and opinions of
the publisher.

British Library Cataloguing-in-Publication Data

A catalogue record for this book is available from the British
Library.

This book and all other Instant Apostle books are available from
Instant Apostle:

Website: www.instantapostle.com

Email: info@instantapostle.com

ISBN 978-1-912726-39-4

Printed in Great Britain.

For my mum, Penelope,
with lots of love

For the coming of the Son of Man (the Messiah) will be just like the days of Noah. For as in those days before the flood they were eating and drinking, marrying and giving in marriage, until the [very] day when Noah entered the ark, and they did not know or understand until the flood came and swept them all away; so will the coming of the Son of Man be [unexpected judgment]. (Matthew 24:37-39)

Contents

Introduction

In January 2008 more than 2,000 tons of wood were washed up on Worthing beach where I live from a cargo ship which sank in a storm.[1] Overnight the stone-strewn shoreline turned into a forest. The scent of pine filled the air, not salt. It was an incredible sight, and what made it even more incredible was the night before, I had watched the movie *Evan Almighty*[2] for the first time.

As I stood on the promenade and looked at all the piles of timber, it literally brought to life the feeling of what it would be like if God told me to build an ark. The timing wasn't coincidental. I believe that's when the Lord planted the seed for me to delve deeper into the ark story and learn more about it.

Though the seed didn't initially sprout, I didn't lose my interest in Noah. And while studying for my Masters in Creative Writing in 2015 the seed started to shoot. I wrote stories and poems centred on the flood, using the Genesis chapters as the source. Thinking creatively about the Bible characters enabled me to explore more about them and I started to become focused on wondering how the women of the ark story felt.

Over the years the Lord hasn't allowed me to forget about Noah and the seed He planted. He has drawn my attention and reminded me in so many different ways, from visiting a

---

[1] 'Washed up timber to be sold off', BBC News, 20th January 2008, news.bbc.co.uk/1/hi/england/7198735.stm (accessed 6th October 2020).
[2] *Evan Almighty*, director Tom Shadyac, Universal Pictures, 2007. God tells a character recently voted into Congress that he needs to build an ark and prepare for a flood.

historical property where an antique Noah's ark model was on display, to a handbag given to me by a friend which had a decoration on it called Noah. Little things, but they reinforced to me that this was something the Lord wanted me to focus on and write about.

I continued to study and think about the story. During the last couple of years I've thought even more about the women who entered the ark. I've realised the issues they faced still resonate for us today. The uncertainty, change, wait, and handling constant new beginnings those four women experienced echo in our lives. The sense of still having to go through circumstances when we don't know exactly what we want to do spoke to me. I also listened to those same concerns from conversations I've had with others as a mentor and friend. Having taken the leap from my leadership role in the UK Civil Service, as I write this book I am once again asking those familiar questions about what steps I take next.

We all have a desire to do something. We all have unique skills and abilities we want to use. We all want to be challenged and grow. And especially when we follow Jesus, we want to serve Him. Unless we're inclined to a certain career path when we're young, such as the vocational call of medicine or teaching, it can be hard during our adult lives to determine what we want to do; even if we have decided, our modern world allows us to change path and retrain. But this sense of *not knowing* perfuses beyond what we do; we can encounter the unknown in many forms.

While I write another unexpected situation occurred with the pandemic in 2020. Though the concept of this book has been in my thoughts for the past years, I hadn't anticipated living through a time when the world would make comparisons to living in 'the days of Noah' (Matthew 24:37). The similarity of being confined to our homes, the feelings of isolation that the pandemic brought into our lives has made people liken the situation to being on the ark. Though some of the understanding and interpretation of the story varies from the truth, such as how long they were on the ark, it's interesting that in difficult times, people thought about Noah and his family.[3]

What we can learn from Noah's story applies even more to our lives, but the book is not just about living through a pandemic. And though I have drawn on some of the similarities to help us understand how the uncertainty, wait and confinement felt for Noah and his family, I want to be careful that we don't confuse the two. Unlike the flood, I don't believe Covid-19 is a judgement from God.

There may be many reasons why you've chosen this book: perhaps the title resonates for you in your circumstances; you're intrigued to understand more about the Noah's ark story; or someone has recommended the book to you. Because I believe in Jesus, and because I believe the flood happened – it isn't just a fictional story or myth – I'm writing this book from my position of faith. Whatever at this point your thoughts are about your own faith, whether you're a Bible-believing Christian or unsure about your relationship with God, my desire is that as we explore the story together, you'll be encouraged to understand more about the hope we have in Him, and how we can not know, but still go.

---

[3] Robert Skidelsky, 'The coronavirus pandemic shows why the West must transform its economic logic', *New Statesman*, 21st April 2020, www.newstatesman.com/politics/economy/2020/04/coronavirus-economics-stockpiling-global-supply-chain (accessed 6th October 2020).

1

Before the Flood

Imagine you live in a village and you stroll along the riverbank where you used to play as a child. Imagine each morning you walk outside, feeling the coolness of the dew-filled grass beneath your bare feet, and look at a cloudless blue sky where the sun always shines. Imagine your three boys have grown up and left your homestead to live with their wives. Imagine your husband telling you one evening in front of the fire that God has spoken to him about a flood.

Imagine you're Emzara: Mrs Noah.

> God said to Noah, 'I intend to make an end of all that lives, for through men the land is filled with violence; and behold, I am about to destroy them together with the land. Make yourself an ark of gopher wood; make in it rooms (stalls, pens, coops, nests, cages, compartments) and coat it inside and out with pitch (bitumen). ... For behold, I, even I, will bring a flood of waters on the earth, to destroy all life under the heavens in which there is the breath *and* spirit of life; everything that is on the land shall die. But I will establish My covenant (solemn promise, formal agreement) with you; and you shall come into the ark – you and your [three] sons and your wife, and your sons' wives with you. And of every living thing [found on land], you shall bring two

of every kind into the ark, to keep them alive with you;
they shall be male and female.'
(Genesis 6:13-14,17-19)[4]

Before Noah started to speak, Emzara might have wondered about what Noah wanted to tell her, but nothing could have prepared her for that conversation – the first time Noah introduced such strange, terrifying and unfamiliar words that God had spoken to him. In that moment any certainty Emzara had about the plans she'd made or the thoughts she had about their future were changed. Something new and unexpected was going to happen. A flood. All life destroyed. Noah was going to build an ark. Only their family would survive.

The words must have reverberated around Emzara's head as she searched for their meaning, to try to make sense of something she had no idea about. In the shock of such news she must have felt disbelief; surely this wasn't really going to happen? Just her, Noah, their sons and daughters-in-law were going to enter an ark, but no one else.

Who were Noah's family?

We know when God spoke to Noah, He made it clear that Noah and his immediate family would be saved. The implications of this news was that it would affect them too; like Emzara, any plans they had made about their lives were also changed.

We may be familiar with the main character of the ark story, Noah, but he also had three sons: Japheth, Shem and Ham (Genesis 5:32). There are different interpretations about who Noah's eldest son was but I think Japheth was the eldest because Genesis 10:21 refers to Shem being 'the brother of Japheth the elder' (NKJV). Genesis 9:24 also tells us that Ham was Noah's younger son so that makes Shem the middle brother.

---

[4] Unless otherwise stated, all bracketed words in Bible quotes are part of the original translation.

Though the Bible tells us who the sons are, we only know their three wives entered the ark. The Bible doesn't identify either their names or the name of Noah's wife; neither does it give us an explanation about why they weren't recorded. Irrespective to their names remaining unknown to us, these four women did exist. They were real.

For the purposes of my book I've named the women to help us as we consider them as characters. I feel doing this enables us to bring their story to life, as we think about the times they lived in and the role they might have played. In the Book of Jubilees,[5] an ancient Jewish text, Emzara is the name given to Noah's wife so I have kept to this. The fictional names I've created for their daughters-in-law are: Tia, the wife of Japheth; Sarah, the wife of Shem; and Mert, the wife of Ham.

I'm not stating their names as fact or intending to alter the Word of God. I believe wholeheartedly everything written within the Bible is God-inspired, infallible and authoritative (see 2 Timothy 3:16). The information we can rely on is contained within the Bible, and it is always this we will return to, as the truth of His Word.

The pre-flood earth

When God spoke to Noah telling him to build an ark, this would have indeed been a surprise. But I don't think the state of the earth would have been a surprise to Noah or Emzara. The Bible is very clear about what the pre-flood earth was like in the days of Noah. When God spoke to Noah about the flood, He told him, 'the land is filled with violence' (Genesis 6:13). All that people could think about was 'evil continually', there were no moral or spiritual standards, and violence was displayed across many forms: blasphemy, law-breaking, the deep need for power (Genesis 6:5,11-12). And we're not just talking about one group

---

[5] Tim Chaffey, 'Who Was Noah's Wife?', Answers in Genesis, 20th January 2015, answersingenesis.org/bible-characters/noah/who-was-noahs-wife/ (accessed 14th October 2020). Used with permission from Answers in Genesis.

of people on the earth here, we're talking about all of the population alive at that time.

We have to remind ourselves the Noah's ark story is in Genesis, the first book of the Bible, and only six chapters into it. Only five chapters since God created the world and thought all of His creation was 'very good' (Genesis 1:31). Since then, humanity had completely imploded into itself, so that during the before-the-flood days, God grieved over the level of sin in the world (Genesis 6:6). When Adam and Eve disobeyed and ate from the tree of knowledge, having been tempted by the serpent (Satan), this fruit gave them the recognition and understanding of what was good and evil (Genesis 2:9; 3:1-7). But despite knowing what good was, and '[the difference between] good and evil' (Genesis 3:5), the majority of people's intentions on the pre-flood earth was only to do evil. They couldn't stop themselves.

What do you think the pre-flood earth looked like? We haven't got any pictures in the Bible. But there are clues that people didn't wander about in an ignorant, nomad state of existence after Adam and Eve left the Garden of Eden. No, the pre-flood earth was a civilised society. Why do I say that?

Adam and Eve's son Cain founded 'a city' (Genesis 4:17). It takes intelligence to think about creating the components, suggesting the formation of buildings being constructed and city-like activities. Also in Genesis 4 it talks about Cain's descendants playing 'the lyre and flute' (Genesis 4:21). They were experts 'in forging tools of bronze and iron' (Genesis 4:22, NLT). We're talking about sophisticated knowledge, both culturally – to create, learn and skilfully produce music on instruments – and industrially – to manufacture tools. Given how the Scriptures talk about violence, I would think they used their metal-working abilities to forge weapons too.

They could have drunk out of gold cups or worn jewellery because one of the rivers flowing from the land of Eden went into Havilah, which is where the purest form of gold was found (Genesis 2:11-12). It's not unlikely, if they knew how to find the materials to work with bronze and iron, that they were able to work gold. They had access to precious onyx stones and resin (Genesis 2:12). Among the population there were construction and agricultural experts.[6] They had to work the ground, which God had cursed after Adam and Eve ate the fruit. Just like farmers have to work hard today to plough, sow and reap their crops, so did the pre-flood farmers.

There would have been a lot of people to feed. Remember that people lived long lifetimes and they were able to raise many children so the population of the pre-flood earth would have been large.[7] Noah was the seventh great grandson of Adam.[8] They lived on an earth that had no rain, where mists watered the soil (Genesis 2:6).

Yet within all of this sophisticated and civilised society, all the hearts of humanity were not given towards godly behaviour. And as the generations from Adam increased and progress was made, we now have, at the time when God spoke to Noah, the peak of lawlessness and the love of self running rife and unrestricted throughout the earth.

Noah and Emzara would have witnessed the change in people's behaviour. Perhaps when Emzara had a chance to reflect on what Noah told her, she was relieved to think they would be escaping the world around them. Living in that kind of environment must have caused her to be in a constant state of fear about the safety for her family. If Emzara had any doubts about what Noah said, the evidence of why God was sending the flood was visible around her. We don't know every evil-filled detail of those pre-flood days, but we do know it was continual evil in all its shades of darkness, and it sorrowed God's heart.

---

[6] John R Rice, *In the Beginning* (Murfreesboro, TN: Sword of the Lord Publishers, 1975), p 169.
[7] Ibid, p 169.
[8] See Genesis 5 for Adam's descendants.

The sorrow of God's heart

When we think of the flood story, it could be easy to misinterpret God's character by trying to understand why everything was destroyed, except the eight people and animals on the ark. But I don't think God made the decision to flood the world lightly at all. He didn't just get annoyed and bang His fist on the table. When God looked at the earth He:

> saw how debased *and* degenerate it was, for all humanity had corrupted their way on the earth *and* lost their true direction.
> (Genesis 6:12)

He was deeply disappointed in people's continual desire to sin and 'that every imagination or intent of the thoughts of his [humanity's] heart were only evil continually' (Genesis 6:5, addition mine). God's heart was sorrowed with grief, and we know sorrow is a strong, tangible emotion. It's a pain we feel. I'm sure we've all experienced this feeling in our lives, and God has too; Genesis tells us this. And now He was going to destroy the people and animals He had created; significantly alter the world He had made through the overwhelming waters. This had never been God's intent because God's heart isn't to destroy. 'God is love' (1 John 4:8). He doesn't have 'pleasure in the death of anyone who dies' (Ezekiel 18:32).

Genesis 2 gives us a picture of what the world would have been like if sin hadn't entered. The Adam and Eve story isn't as simple as them eating an apple; it's about the serpent, Satan (Genesis 3:1), otherwise known as the devil, Lucifer, the dragon, the enemy, who robbed us of that perfect relationship with God by lying to Eve. Humanity fell once the fruit was eaten. The world couldn't veer off the self-destructive, sinful path it had led itself to; not even Noah could save it. And the only reason he could save himself and his family was because God told him to build an ark.

How did the family react?

We can only imagine how Noah and Emzara shared the news with their sons and daughters-in-law. Perhaps they all came to the homestead for a family meal, anticipating a time to enjoy being with each other. Instead, strange words again filled the air. Did Sarah start to cry? Did Tia interrupt and ask lots of questions? Did Mert storm out? Had Noah already told his sons so they could comfort their wives and weren't in shock themselves?

Tia, Sarah and Mert had married into the family. They had been given protection against the flood's judgement because Noah was their father-in-law. There must have been relief that their lives would be saved, but coupled with this would have come the guilt that no one else they knew would survive. And what of their own families? Even if Tia had rushed to her mother, told her all about what Noah had said, she wouldn't have got the consolation she sought. Her mother and all her other relatives would have been consumed in their own schemes. No one would believe judgement was coming. The darkness was so thick and immense that they wouldn't even be able to spot a glimmer of light. No, Tia, Sarah and Mert surely couldn't rely on their families for any solace; seeing them would be a reminder about what they'd be leaving behind.

Let's take a step back here. We know how the ark story ended; we've read or can read Genesis. But did the women?

No.

All they knew was the beginning. I don't think we can minimise at all how difficult it must have been for them to comprehend the fact they would enter the ark, but no one else would. I'll say that again: *no one else on the earth was going to go with them.* No parents, no siblings, no best friend, not even Noah's father, Lamech. And Lamech had prophesied when he named his son, about the 'rest *and* comfort' Noah would bring (Genesis 5:29), but he wasn't going to experience it himself. Whoever was alive at the time when the flood came would be destroyed.

Though it was only Noah who heard God speak to him, the result of those words was that Noah's family unit were gathered in tightly together. Among the sin-stained world, where 'all humanity had corrupted their way on the earth *and* lost their true direction' (Genesis 6:12), were eight people. They were the only eight people who knew the flood was coming. The only eight people who would survive, and 50 per cent of them were women.

The unfamiliar and unexpected

There are many times in our lives when we feel that nervous jolt from doing things we aren't completely sure about. The first driving lesson. Taking an exam. Meeting strangers. Walking into a building we've never been in before for an interview. When we do these things, along with the feeling of the unfamiliar comes some confidence of certainty. We can reassure ourselves internally with messages that we've experienced *something* like this before. We can prepare and research. We can say, 'This may not be the same, but I'll get through it. I did it before, I can do it again.'

After Noah shared with Emzara the unexpected news about the flood, how could she reassure herself? Everything she knew and had lived through gave her nothing concrete to centre her emotions on to. Nothing to give her a solution to the wave of emotions she must have felt. She couldn't pick up her mobile phone and search for what an ark looked like. In a moment, her life switched from the regular routines of the ordinary into the sudden extraordinary, with Noah chopping down gopher-tree-filled forests to build an ark for a flood, which she had never experienced, let alone seen.

Can you imagine the kinds of questions Emzara must have had? If it was me, I would have asked Noah, 'When exactly is the flood going to happen? Sorry, but did you say animals were going to live with us? What does a flood look like?' Noah, though, wouldn't have had the answers to these questions.

I think it's natural when we come across something we don't know about to want to ask lots of questions. In our helplessness at the situation we seek to have some form of knowledge. I am someone who likes to know all the details. My instinct is to explore, prepare, check things out, think through all the scenarios. Essentially what we're doing, though, when we act this way, is wanting to control our circumstances, but this isn't always possible, neither is it restful for our state of mind. Particularly when we're greeted with the unexpected, and we can't immediately solve it, we're unable to know how to react. The reality of the unexpected is that we can't know everything. We can't have all our questions answered.

The world was thrown into such an unfamiliar situation in 2020, when for the first time in our lives we were all experiencing the unexpected – invisible virus. We all, like Noah and his family, heard strange, new words, which would have seemed unfathomable a year earlier. We couldn't understand what everything meant. There was no immediate solution. There weren't answers to all our questions. We had to learn to adapt what we did to protect each other and ourselves. Our daily lives became dictated by something unprecedented in our lifetime. Decisions made by our governments determined how we lived and what we could and couldn't do. There were, and continue to be, so many impacts across the world as a result of what lay behind those virus-related words that entered our lives and affected them.

How do we not send ourselves into emotional chaos?

The unexpected we're thinking about here isn't like when there's a rain shower and we can put up an umbrella. It isn't easily resolvable. Beside the shocking times we have experienced with the pandemic, there are many forms of the unfamiliar and unexpected that manifest in our lives. And we know the strength of our emotional reaction when we encounter them; when we can't see our way out of the maze and there are no directions.

We can cripple ourselves with the desire to control the unexpected; our natural attempts to solve the problem in front of us. In those times when I've felt helpless, I've made impetuous decisions based on my feelings in the moment. I've let worry slump me into the sofa so I end up comforting myself with cake. I've thought I've made myself happy, and then something small has snapped it away, like a crocodile sneaking up silently for its prey.

So, what can we do when we don't see any answers? When there is no hope around us?

Though we may feel numb and exhausted from the storm of emotions, we still have each day to live through, and we may ask, like David did, 'What am I doing in the meantime, Lord? *Hoping*, that's what I'm doing – hoping' (Psalm 39:7, *The Message*). The kind of hope David was speaking of here isn't the power of positive thinking, because that relies on our mental strength, and in the emotional chaos, mental strength can be something we lack. It relies on *our* efforts to try to solve *our* problems.

However, there is another way out; the hope through our faith in the Lord. This enables us to say, 'For my hope is from Him. He only is my rock and my salvation' (Psalm 62:5-6). We can stand firm on it and, while there may be no confidence in anything around us, we can be confident in the hope He gives us.

We are indeed not hopeless but hopeful in Him.

So what did the women do?

After Emzara's conversation with Noah, she still had all those unanswered questions; the emotional reactions which wouldn't have been easy to process. All I think she could do was work with what she knew. Though they didn't have all the information, they weren't completely ignorant. They knew a flood was coming. They knew the ark needed to be built. They knew a pair of every living thing would enter. These were the things that among all of the uncertainty she could focus on.

Then, as Noah set out and began to cut the trees down in the forests, hewing the trunks into planks, it gave a visible daily reminder of the purpose God had given him. Did Emzara wonder what her purpose was within all of this too? Among all the pain and suffering, the weight of knowing what was to come and not being able to do anything to change it, I believe God's love had a plan for the women. God saved them for a purpose; they weren't an afterthought.

We may question God's love among the extent of destruction and death that the flood brought to the earth. But it was God's love that chose not to eradicate humanity completely, and God's love would have considered the human lives who'd be taking that ark journey.

The Bible doesn't tell us what the women did. They could have sat and watched everything going on from the sidelines, waiting until the day Noah told them they could enter the ark. Though, if we think about the characteristics of women, I can't imagine them *not doing anything*. God had given Noah an enormous task. He didn't just have to build the ark, but he also had to prepare for their time aboard:

> Also take with you every kind of food that is edible, and you shall collect *and* store it; and it shall be food for you and for them.
> (Genesis 6:21)

Remember there were no timescales here. Noah didn't know whether he had ten years or ten months until the flood. So though at first this verse sounds straightforward, is it really?

Food is an important part of our lives; we need to eat to live. We have to think about what we're going to eat. We may plan meals and manage the money we spend on food. Rewind, though. God has told Noah to collect and store food not only for his family, but also for 'every living thing [found on land]'

(Genesis 6:19). And rewind even more. Did God say anywhere how long they were going to be on the ark? No.

Think about times when the shops are closed over national holidays. We see some people panic, buying essential supplies so they know they have enough, and that's just when the shop is closed for one day! But for Noah and his family, we're talking about enough provisions for a journey with no end date.

I can't imagine Emzara not wanting to support Noah with this tremendous task. When he told the family about all of the food he had to collect and store, wouldn't it have been the women who would have had the experience of managing the meals for their households? Who would have had an understanding of the quantities and varieties of dishes to prepare? Wouldn't it be them who would at least be cooking some of the food on the ark?

Then, what about the food for all the animals? Considering all the different kinds of food for all the different kinds of creatures they'd be caring for…

Somehow I don't think Noah could have done it all on his own.

I think this is where the women could have stepped in and found their purpose. Maybe focusing on doing something necessary and constructive helped them with the turmoil of emotions brought from the unknown? As they entered the before-the-flood phase, the women had to go about their daily lives, while being conscious of the future change they all faced. They had to be productive in their preparations. It wouldn't have been a case of packing a sack of dried fruit one day and then leaving the work for a couple of weeks. They'd have had to think about what moths ate. Experiment with storage methods. Determine how many cucumbers would need to be grown and pickled. Picture Emzara as she woke in the middle of the night to the sound of Noah snoring, with the thought, 'How many jars of olive oil will we need?'

I believe Emzara, Tia, Sarah and Mert would have all had skills and abilities to manage and organise, plan and prepare, think creatively and problem solve; all of these would have a crucial part to play. And among the action, among Emzara's constant checking of the tasks assigned to each of her daughters-in-law, would have still been the uncertainty. God had told Noah to collect and store food, but He hadn't given Noah the same level of detail for that as He did for the ark's specifications. All the women could do was work with what they knew.

Whatever their expectation had been for their lives, whatever the women thought their purpose was, it had shifted. And with this transition came the enormity of the challenge, the environment of the pre-flood earth and their own personal emotional reactions. As the ark was built, days turned into weeks, then into years, and any jars of pickled vegetables would have had to be eaten before they wasted – the day of the flood hadn't yet come. Produce needed to be grown and harvested. The women would have had to continue to motivate and support each other because they wouldn't know until the flood came whether they had done enough.

Working with what you know

When we think about how the women might have handled the before-the-flood days, don't we frequently find ourselves having to do that – work with what we know?

This sounds similar to how I feel and how I've felt many times before. I have something to do in front of me, but it isn't clear; I only know a piece of the picture. Sometimes, whatever that piece is, it feels or appears so small that at first it can be hard to even begin.

There is a difference between having a vision of what we're doing in our lives and the energy that gives us, and the times when we struggle and find ourselves looking back, thinking we've lost our momentum. With no discernible goal in front of us it's so easy to diminish the *what we know work* our hands have found to do against what we think they must be doing, or what we've done before.

Through the coronavirus pandemic, I had to learn to literally take each day at a time. To try to not drive myself into the chaotic state of mind created by thinking about what would happen. The truth is, I'm not superhuman. I wasn't able to do any of this on my own. If I didn't have Jesus in my life helping me, I know those months would have been even tougher with the level of anxiety the situation caused. But Jesus was with me, comforting me, filling me with the indescribable, unexplainable sense of peace that only comes from a relationship with Him. He helped me to understand even more what He meant when He said, 'So do not worry about tomorrow; for tomorrow will worry about itself. Each day has enough trouble of its own' (Matthew 6:34).

It's easy to read this verse and agree, but to apply it in your life when you're faced with the unexpected and unfamiliar isn't easy. Jesus isn't surprised by how we think or feel, though; that's why He knows we need His hope. And that's why He advised us not to use up all our energy and time worrying about what might happen tomorrow, even though He knows we want to do that!

This doesn't mean we're in the wrong if we find ourselves worrying or thinking about what's ahead, but if we dwell on those thoughts, let them overtake us so we're consumed, it's not going to be good. As Jesus said, it's not going to help us focus on any actual troubles which may face us on the day we're living in if we're worrying already about the next.

Emotions are strong and wonderful, a blessing and a burden. But don't let your strength be sapped by them. The only answer we have to all those unexpected questions that arise, to the emotional chaos that could affect us in a crisis, is to turn to Jesus. He wants us to cast our cares on to Him (1 Peter 5:7). He wants us to have confidence in His hope.

*Father, thank You that You know the beginning and the end.
Let me draw confidence in Your plans, understanding that,
despite all the uncertainty that came when You spoke to Noah
about the flood, You gave him and his family enough
information to help them with the task at hand. Fill me with
the hope only You can supply. Help me to work with what I
know when the unexpected and unfamiliar happens in my life.
Help me today with the worries I have, with all those thoughts
swirling around my head about what will be in my unexpected.
I want to offload my burden into Your capable hands.
Amen.*

Before we move on, let's take some time to think. Here are some suggestions to help you and, as we go through, there will be contemplation points at the end of each chapter. If, like me, you like writing down your thoughts, you can either use the next couple of pages or your own journal. Otherwise, feel free to express your thinking in whichever way works best for you.

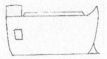

Chapter contemplations

- Familiarise yourself with where we are in the Bible and read through Genesis chapters 1–5, which lead to the flood.

- Think about how you would feel if you were one of the women, and write down any thoughts in your journal.

- Reflect on past times when you've experienced the unexpected and how you've handled it.

Journal pages

2

If Noah Was a People Pleaser, Then He Wouldn't Have Built the Ark

What kind of reception did Noah receive from people outside his family when he told them about the flood? As he earnestly started building the ark, did people wonder what he was doing and ask? When he told them, surely he would have been met with disbelief? People laughing at the thought of a flood destroying the earth when not even a drop of rain fell from the sky in those days? Despite Noah's trust in God's word, there must have been the temptation to satisfy friends or other family members so he and his family would be accepted and liked. They might have felt a need to reach out to someone else for confirmation that what they were doing was right, even if they knew in their hearts no one else would give it to them. The reality is that if Noah or his family had chosen to try to keep the people around them happy, rather than listen to what God had told Noah, there would have been a completely different ending to the ark story.

Why do we want to ask others?

Though there may be times when we want to live on an island away from everyone, we are social people. We need interactions with each other. We like to feel part of a group or team. The growth of social media and online communities is all about people finding connections and conversing about similar interests.

So it isn't surprising that when things happen in our lives, we go to others. Whenever we have good or bad news, what do we do? We want to share. We want that celebratory high five or a hug. When we're either taking a new directional course or craving to know where we need to go, it isn't surprising that we look to people to confirm or tell us what to do.

This can be especially during those times when:

- the horizon blurs and we can't see the bigger picture;

- we haven't got enough information to guide us into our next step; or

- doubt fills our mind about the direction we sense God is prompting us to take.

All of these can make us feel lost. I think when we feel lost it's a natural human instinct to want help. After all, how many times when we're driving somewhere new do we seek advice about our route? Whether this is rolling down the car window and asking someone out walking their dog or using the satnav app on our smartphone, we want to check we're going in the right direction.

There is a difference, though, between reassurance that we're heading in the right direction and relying on others to tell us where to go. But if we do want others to constantly approve of our actions, then aren't we giving control of our life to them?

You need everyone else around you to confirm that you've made the right decision. You feel like you don't know how to get yourself out of a situation and you want someone, anyone, to tell you what to do. You want to move forward so much and you want a person to say, 'Go this way; do that thing.' Sound familiar? Yes, me too. I'm raising my hand here.

Emzara must have wanted to talk things through with a close friend. But then, how do you ask a close friend for their thoughts about your situation when you're telling them at the same time that the whole earth is going to be destroyed, including them? Even if Emzara thought she could have discussed the ark in the hope it might convict her friend, in the hope it might lift the blindfold and help her friend to seek good rather than wrongdoing, what if it didn't? I expect Emzara would have been scorned by her friend, who would reject her for believing in something as crazy and foolish as a flood. Then would have come the temptation for Emzara to laugh along and agree, to change her conviction, so in that brief moment she'd see a smile of acceptance on her friend's face. But I hope Emzara wasn't a people pleaser.

What does people pleasing mean?

Let's just review the definition of people pleasing for a moment. A people pleaser is:

> someone who cares a lot about whether other people like them, and always wants others to approve of their actions.[9]

The words 'cares a lot' and 'always wants others to approve' stand out to me in the definition. That's the difference between a person who doesn't depend on what people think about them and someone who constantly relies on others' affirmation.

---

[9] Definition of people pleaser from Cambridge Dictionary, www.dictionary.cambridge.org, © Cambridge University Press. Used with permission. Reproduced with permission of the Licensor through PLSclear.

I think that approval we seek when we people please is linked to our own sense of self-worth and self-esteem. Often when we people please we don't get any sustained benefit from what we do and it can go against who we are. However, the momentary reward we get from a person's approval, the feeling of being accepted, makes us feel better. Our desire for others to increase how we value ourselves overrides our sense of judgement. It clouds our ability to think. So, being busy people pleasing everyone else means we don't have to focus on what's going on with us. Do we think it's wrong to think about ourselves?

Would I say I'm a people pleaser? I don't want to admit it, but yes. I've definitely done things I shouldn't because of the wrong motivation, said 'Yes' to so many different types of questions and then wondered why I've committed myself to something.

It feels awkward to say you're a people pleaser, because though many of us will do some form of people pleasing in our lives, it's not something we want to own. When we know we're doing it we perceive it as a kind of weakness because we're going against how we feel inside. We think we're not strong enough to say or act how we really feel.

I think we need to be gentle with ourselves, though. There are many drivers that lead to people pleasing behaviour and it's the kind of behaviour which easily becomes a habit. It's hard to identify we're craving approval in the moment, so we can't stop ourselves. Usually it's only afterwards that we realise what we've done... Plus, when we behave in this way, we often find people like us even more because we're one of those people who'll do things. If we're at a meeting and the leader asks for help, it's usually those people who always say 'Yes' that they look to first. There have been many times I've taken on extra projects out of the wrong motives. It's tough, isn't it?

Saying 'Yes' to things doesn't mean you're a chronic people pleaser, but you do need to ask yourself about what you're doing. And that requires some uncomfortable self-analysis.

The need to be right

About seven years ago, I had a promotion opportunity at work. I'd known for a while I needed to move on within the organisation and have a new challenge, but I wasn't quite sure what that was. An opportunity arose, and it all happened rather quickly from the application process to interview, resulting in a job offer that was based in London.

At first I was so happy when I got the job offer, I knew in my spirit[10] from the Holy Spirit that it was good, even though it would bring a lot of change. Then I discovered that though my role was changing location, the train fares wouldn't be covered by the business. Happiness quickly converted into fear and worry. Money turned into an overriding factor, which hadn't been in my thinking when I'd applied. I worried about how I'd pay the extra travel costs to commute from my home town to London. There was a slight wage increase from the promotion but it didn't provide enough for the travel. Looking back I can see how Satan wanted to rob me; I lost my peace. The enemy[11] didn't know what my future looked like, but he was going to try his best to stop me from entering into it.

My attention switched from God who makes all things possible (Matthew 19:26) to whether *I* could make all things possible. The money problem then flicked another big fear switch about whether the decision I'd made was right. Satan can play a good game, and he knew if he got me thinking about whether I was right, about whether this was the right thing for me to do, he'd get me twisted into knots because he knew he had from past experiences.

It sure worked. I went to colleagues. I asked my friends. I felt confused. I couldn't stop turning things over in my mind.

---

[10] It says in 1 Thessalonians 5:23, we have a spirit, soul and body. When we give our lives to Jesus, we're born again (John 3:3) and our spiritual life in Him is birthed. We receive the Holy Spirit who 'testifies *and* confirms together with our spirit [assuring us] that we [believers] are children of God' (Romans 8:16). The Holy Spirit's leading is what we sense in our spirit.

[11] When I talk about the enemy, I'm not referring to a person, but Satan.

I'm not sure what my new manager thought as my emails went from accepting the job to an email where I actually ended up turning the job down. It had got to that point. But even refusing the opportunity, therefore taking away the problem of the commuting costs, didn't make me happy. What did I do next? I went to everyone else to confirm whether that decision was right!

Around that time I went to a Christian event. I can remember feeling so heavy and oppressed. There was a prayer time at the end, and I was so desperate I went forward for ministry. I shared with a lady about my circumstances, my indecision apparent, as I explained the scenario to her. Once I finished, she prayed with me, and then said, 'There is no right answer.' Those words may not sound significant, but for me at that time those five words were God-given.

I compare receiving prayer ministry to peeling an onion. Sometimes God brings healing and resolution into our lives at once; other times, He gently peels off layer by layer, to help us mend and deal with issues, as we move through life. This was one of those times.

So having that knowledge, 'there is no right answer', simple as it might have been, helped me to understand there wasn't a right answer in the fear-fuelled storm the enemy had caused me to create. If the 'right answer' had been to turn down the job and therefore have no financial loss, then why was I still restless? That wasn't the 'right' answer. All of that worry and self-doubt, seeking people's approval or direction as to what was right, had completely overshadowed the bubble of joy in my spirit I'd initially felt. That's what I returned to, and I'm so grateful to the Lord because He is the God who makes all things possible. In spite of all my vacillations and what Satan tried to do, the job was still there. I was able to accept it, again!

What happened to those worries about the money? The Lord provided through an unexpected bonus to help with the first few months' travel costs, and I had peace about the rest. Yes, I might have had to be financially careful at the start, but

I never lacked. More than that, there came so many unforeseen blessings through the job opportunity and how my career progressed.

The Lord used the situation to help me understand more about myself, and I learned more about trusting in Him too. I haven't completely lost the need-to-be-right feeling, but when it arises I'm able to identify and bring it to Him so Satan can't push the button. Indeed, the Lord does make 'all things work together for [our] good' (Romans 8:28, NKJV, addition mine).

Some other ways we can people please

Alongside wanting people's approval or letting them lead us when we don't know which way to go, there are other occasions when we can people please.

We're scared of people
I've found from thinking about my own behaviour that sometimes this desire to people please comes from being afraid. What do I mean? I mean that we don't have confidence in who we are to say 'No'. And then when we say 'No', we over-scrutinise why we've said it or worry about how it may affect people's acceptance of us.

Words can make us react physically. We cry when we watch a sad movie scene. We get hungry – well, I do – if a character in a book eats cake. There will be people in our lives who can hurt us with their words. We're scared of their reaction. In these circumstances it feels easier to please them to avoid the confrontation, because then we won't get hurt. And if we're wired like this, we may find any kind of encounter hard, such as telling a person in a restaurant about a bad meal; we don't want to make a scene.

The Message translation of Proverbs 29:25 explains it well: 'The fear of human opinion disables; trusting in GOD protects you from that.' Fear isn't always based on truth. What we're doing when we're afraid of the potential clash is making an anticipatory judgement about what will happen. We're so afraid of the *potential* reaction, we can't say no or be graciously honest about what we want to say. Maybe someone overreacted when we didn't people please in the past so we assume this will always be the case. We may have experienced violence in our lives, so even the thought of having words like weapons hit us is too much. We've experienced so much pain already that we want to protect ourselves, so it's easier just to go along with and please them rather than having to handle the confrontation.

When the Proverbs 29:25 verse speaks about 'trusting in GOD', I don't think this is a passive trust. We can't just say, 'I won't be afraid again,' and think that's it, we'll get the protection. The reality is we have a tendency to feel afraid. I know I still do. So it means we have to actively trust God. To ask Him to help us. To ask Him in each circumstance when we're tempted to people please, especially when we're scared. Trusting in Him means we're solely relying on the acceptance we have through Him so we don't crave or need acceptance from anyone else. We then don't people please out of fear because we know and have come to understand the perfect love from Him (1 John 4:18).

We don't want to get into a verbal war
There are times when if we say what we want then there's going to be a reaction. We're going to get into an argument.

Is this more a case of thinking about how we are going to respond rather than ignoring how we feel? Are we being wise not opening ourselves up to a verbal tirade? How can we not people please to avoid confrontation?

Thinking about Noah, he was at serious risk of getting into many wars of words during those ark-building days. People wouldn't have believed him, therefore every conversation could have led to a stand-off. Hopefully Noah was more intent on trying to save people from the flood's judgement rather than getting into disagreements.

Thinking about our words, Paul says, 'Let your speech at all times be gracious *and* pleasant' (Colossians 4:6). This is echoed in Proverbs 16:24: 'Pleasant words are like a honeycomb.' So is there a way to be both gracious and honest? It isn't about conceding who's right or wrong, but it's about having wisdom to be considerate in the words we speak. 'A gentle answer deflects anger, but harsh words make tempers flare' (Proverbs 15:1, NLT).

We don't want to cause offence

This could be a friend asking us for an opinion on a new outfit they've bought. What do we say if we think it doesn't suit them? Do we lie – after all, it's just a little white lie – and say it looks good? Or do we tell them the truth?

How we reply will depend on the kind of relationship we have with our friend. It may be tempting to not tell the truth – we want to please them – but when we lie, it leaks out. Our body language gives us away, our friend knows we didn't really mean it, and if we lie even out of jest, it's still wounding:

> Just as damaging as a madman shooting a deadly weapon is someone who lies to a friend and then says, 'I was only joking.'
> (Proverbs 26:18-19, NLT)

When we lie because we don't want to cause offence, it chips away at us. It creates a falseness about who we are. This doesn't mean our words have to be harsh; telling the truth can still be sweet.

It also comes back to whether our view or opinion on a matter will alter people's acceptance of us. This is hard when we live in an age with information that doesn't agree with our biblical faith. We can face a barrage of criticism on social media if we state something that goes against popular thinking. We might be inclined to 'like' or agree with something because we think it's easier. Are we 'trying to win the favor *and* approval of men, or of God' (Galatians 1:10)?

'Integrity' feels like an appropriate word to say here. Why? Because this all relates to the integrity we have from God. We may have our own moral integrity but this is about following biblical principles. And we don't just get this kind of integrity as a free upgrade when we become Christians. It's something that we learn and apply from the wisdom of His Word. We may not deliberately seek to offend, but we may also have to be brave and not be afraid to state or speak out our views:

> Let your eyes look directly ahead [toward the path of moral courage]
> And let your gaze be fixed straight in front of you [toward the path of integrity].
> (Proverbs 4:25)

It's a decision to keep our eyes looking straight ahead, to not let ourselves be led into those situations where we get sidetracked and people please instead. When we look towards the Lord, this is what gives us the courage to sensitively speak the truth while not hurting others (Ephesians 4:25).

Destiny

As I've reflected on the ark story, I've realised there is another time when I find myself going to people for guidance, and this is when I'm not sure whether I'm fulfilling my destiny, whether I'm achieving enough. Funny how it feels easier during those times to ask people rather than ask God. I think words like 'destiny' can be dangerous. They conjure up thoughts of heroic stories or a mystical idea about what fulfilling our destiny means.

When we think of destiny, it gives a feeling that our future is out of our hands – we don't control it. This ties in with when we think of fate or luck, that what happens in life is by chance. The roll of a dice. The unseen force determining whether we win or lose.

Have we got ourselves confused between what the world measures and believes in as destiny and what the Bible tells us?

Have we, in our desire to be of the world, to go about our daily lives and succeed here, blurred the boundaries between being obedient to what God wants us to do and the world's expectations? And does this worldly expectation about destiny centre on wanting to know the future? That feeling of needing to push through and succeed? To beat the odds? Perhaps we want to believe in our power to shape our destiny?

Let's press the mute button, though, because this is starting to sound like it's coming from the world's speaker. Control your own destiny. You have the power. You can change your future. Self-belief. Self-knowledge. Me-me-me-me-me. Who needs God when we can do everything ourselves? Right?

Wrong. So very wrong.

What is our destiny? For those of us who have given our lives to God, who have chosen a new life in Him, through Jesus dying for us on the cross, we don't need to be preoccupied about what our future is. We don't need to have our fortune told. We have security, we have eternal life with Him, that's our ultimate destiny. In the meantime, as David wrote in Psalm 23, we have a Shepherd walking alongside us, who wants to help guide us through the mountains and valleys. So we can say, 'Surely goodness and mercy *and* unfailing love shall follow me all the days of my life' (Psalm 23:6).

What about purpose?

When we think about destiny, it's natural the next word that comes to mind is 'purpose'. We've already thought about the change of purpose the women might have felt with the news of the flood. Did Noah consider building the ark to be his purpose? There aren't any verses in the Bible about Noah or any of his family crying out, 'I'm fulfilling my purpose!' Instead, Genesis says, 'Noah did ... all that God commanded him' (Genesis 6:22). He got on with it without the need for a fanfare.

There's a link between purpose and motivation. When we purpose to do something, we find this gives energy. I find this particularly if I purpose to make a chocolate brownie! Our bigger purposes often require us to have vision of the goal in sight – that's what gives us the determination to pursue them. Perhaps you're saying at this point, 'I don't have a goal,' or, 'I don't even know what my purpose is or what I should be doing.' I get that.

We feel this weight throughout our lives, that we need to know what we want to do. I think this can be instilled in us from when we're children, when we're always asked, 'What do you want to be when you grow up?' Yes, growing up requires us to think about study, work, a career, but it creates an awareness of people having expectations that we'll know what we want to do with our lives, when often that is far from the truth. Five-year plans, three-year plans, bucket lists, even New Year's resolutions reinforce this idea that we need to be purposeful and achieve lots of goals.

How does that help me, you might ask?

Well, purpose is good. If, like Noah, we're given a clear task to do, or if we feel a peace to commit ourselves to achieve something, such as learning to drive or changing career, that's not wrong, we have that focus in sight. But then neither are those times wrong when we feel like we're searching for goals we can't find. God does have a purpose for our lives. He may not write it across the skies. We may not know exactly what the whole pie is going to look like, but we shouldn't defeat ourselves before we've started making the pastry. There is hope in the small things, so when God whispers something that you may measure as tiny-to-do-today, don't demean it in the search for the achievement. The visible accomplishment. Don't make yourself feel insignificant about your daily victories by comparing them against what others might think.

We can be assured and have confidence in God. He loves us, and He hasn't just told us how much, but He's also shown us with the most precious gift He could give, the life of His only Son, Jesus.

You may ask, 'So as God gave His Son's life for me, then why won't He help me to understand those next goals?' He doesn't want us to be afraid or feel like failures; He doesn't want us to rely on others to tell us what our purpose is – we need to talk to Him. Again it comes back to trusting and believing in His promises for us, for He is the 'God who will fulfill his purpose for me' (Psalm 57:2, NLT).

A final thought

People pleasing comes down to choosing who we listen to and what we place as important. It is easy to be swayed by the many different voices around us. How can we listen to those world-influenced voices which fill our lives and what the Bible says?

You can't listen to rap and classical music at the same time. Noah couldn't pick and choose. He had to stay focused while he sawed another plank of wood. Noah might have been good at making a fence, but he didn't choose to sit on one. So don't be afraid to change your behaviour and habits, with the Lord's help. We don't need to pinch ourselves to know that we currently live in the world. But we don't belong here, so we don't need to worry about pleasing it. We aren't part of this world; Jesus says, 'I have chosen you out of the world' (John 15:19).

Whether we do what people ask because we're scared of them or if we take a certain course of action because we want the blessing of someone's approval, we mustn't feel guilty. We can't just say, 'I'm not going to people please.' It doesn't work like that. We might be able to manage for a very little while but we'll fail in our own efforts. This is where we need to be able to learn, identify and understand those weaknesses – and, crucially, bring them to Jesus. You know God isn't surprised about this. He created us. We're not robots; He wants to help us. Don't allow Satan to press any buttons of shame, to make you feel like you'll never measure up. If you people pleased five minutes ago,

God still loves you the same right now as He did yesterday. He never changes (Malachi 3:6).

I'm not suggesting that in our walk with the Lord we don't ask others. There are lots of scriptures about godly wisdom, and I do believe in each season of life we go through God gives us people to counsel and guide us. God knows we need that personal interaction: 'Where *there is* no counsel, the people fall; But in the multitude of counselors *there is* safety' (Proverbs 11:14, NKJV).

The verse could refer to the wider sense of guidance given through a nation's leader, or a pastor. But I think we also need wise counsellors in our lives. We need people we can talk with. Having said that, we also need to weigh and measure, test and consider the counsel we receive. Over and above what others say, we should be going to Jesus. Let's have a conversation with Him first. If He wants to use wise counsel from others, we'll know it. We'll feel it confirming what's in our spirit, feel the perfect peace that only comes from Him. And if we don't get any answer from Jesus in the morning, then we won't put everything into what a friend says in the afternoon because Jesus hasn't got back to us sooner. In our relationship with Jesus we need to trust and wait.

Emzara, Tia, Sarah and Mert were given a fresh purpose with everything they had to do before entering the ark, but still during all those days of preparation they didn't know everything. We don't know everything, but: 'The LORD says, "I will guide you along the best pathway for your life. I will advise you and watch over you"' (Psalm 32:8, NLT).

This means we're to be considerate about what we say and do. We don't fill our time with everything that pleases everyone else but doesn't really please us, or what the Lord may want us to do with our time instead.

So in those moments of uncertainty about where to go or what to do, we don't rush impetuously just because someone told us a great idea. What we need to do in those times is to rush back to God. Jesus is the only person who can give us perfect peace about our situation and what steps we need to take:

> Peace I leave with you; My [perfect] peace I give to you; not as the world gives do I give to you. Do not let your heart be troubled, nor let it be afraid. [Let My perfect peace calm you in every circumstance and give you courage and strength for every challenge.]
> (John 14:27)

Like Noah, who chose to obey the Lord despite everything the world said, let's encourage ourselves, knowing that as we've given our lives to Jesus, we have chosen who we serve (Joshua 24:15). He will be faithful to us. Before we know it, through obeying Him each day with the small things, we will move forward, we will make progress, even when we can't feel it.

> *Father, thank You for knowing me and accepting me where I am today. Your love for me remains the same whether I change my people pleasing behaviour or not. Father, I do need Your help to change, and I want to, because I want that closer relationship with You. I don't want to rely on human voices telling me the direction I should go or confirming my decisions. I don't want to be busy so that others will like me, when they should like me for who I am in You. I long for your quiet, still, soothing voice. The voice that belongs to my Father with whom all things are possible.[12] It feels hard, Lord, to do nothing, especially when I don't know Your purpose. But I trust in Your purpose for me. Help me to learn to rely on Your wisdom, so that I don't*

---

[12] Matthew 19:26.

seek guidance from the world. Let me rest in Your presence and let Your peace be the lamp that guides my way.[13]
Amen.

---

[13] Psalm 119:105.

Chapter contemplations

- Do you have a tendency to people please? You find yourself doing things for the wrong reasons and perhaps even paying a price for agreeing to do them? Ask the Lord for His strength to change. Learn about yourself, so that with His grace, you can stop before you lead yourself down the people pleasing path.

- Look up the definitions of 'destiny' and 'purpose'. Note in your journal their similarities and differences. How do these compare to what the Bible says about them? Start by reading Romans 8:30 and Philippians 4:13.

- Remind yourself, when worldly voices try to divert you, that you don't need their approval. Believe the Lord will bring wise, trusted friends and counsellors into your life, but pursue His voice to be your ultimate guide.

Journal pages

3
Favour and Grace

Among all of the people living on the earth before the flood, it can be hard for us to comprehend why Noah was chosen to build the ark and his family were spared God's judgement.

So what was Noah like?

We've already identified that the world Noah lived in was corrupt and putrid, thick and dark in its evilness. Despite all of the lives of everyone living at that time, only one flame flickered. That flame was Noah. The Bible doesn't tell us how many offerings Noah made, the colour of his hair or the size of his homestead. The Bible doesn't tell us about everything he did, but it does tell us about Noah's character:

> Noah was a righteous man [one who was just and had right standing with God], blameless in his [evil] generation; Noah walked (lived) [in habitual fellowship] with God.
> (Genesis 6:9)

Against the backdrop of how society was at this time, we can see why Noah stood out. Noah must have stood out not only to God, but also to those around, in how he conducted himself. Here we're told he was 'blameless' in his generation; this means he was innocent and not guilty of any of the examples of evil behaviour. While those around him entrenched themselves more into choosing to act this way, Noah didn't. We've talked before about the fruit Adam and Eve ate in the Garden of Eden, and how it gave them the knowledge of 'good and evil' (Genesis 3:5). So though Noah knew what good and evil was, he chose good.

Thinking of 'being good' brings up images of telling children, 'Now be good, don't fight over the toys,' or when we're trying to be *really good* and not eat any unhealthy snacks. But we're talking here about Noah choosing goodness at a deeper level, not just 'being good' and having to try really hard to keep at it. Perhaps Noah was blameless because of some of the other characteristics Genesis 6:9 reveals? Let's explore this some more.

Noah was a righteous man

In addition to telling us Noah was righteous, the Amplified Bible breaks this down, adding, '[one who was just and had right standing with God]'. What is this 'right standing'? Somehow I don't think this is a reference to Noah's posture.

'Right standing' could make us think of the people we refer to who have a standing in our communities. If we need our identity verified for official papers, often our documents are witnessed by someone who is a lawyer, teacher or another kind of professional. It theoretically means they are people who are trusted, and who have a good reputation. However, I think there's more going on within the verse because there is a definite correlation between 'right standing' and righteous, and what gives us the link are two crucial words: 'with God'. So though Noah had morals, was fair and just, would indeed have been a person of 'right standing' in his community, we're also talking about righteousness, which only comes *with God*. Being made righteous through Him.

Noah was the only man like this in his generation, but when we explore Noah's genealogy it helps us to understand that there were others in his family who had been righteous with

God before. We know from Genesis 5 that Noah was descended from Seth. Seth was Adam and Eve's third son who was born after Cain murdered Abel.

Later on in Seth's offspring we're told that Noah's great-grandfather, Enoch, walked 'in habitual fellowship' with God and he did this with 'reverent fear and obedience' (Genesis 5:22,24). It's interesting that Genesis tells us about Enoch's relationship with God and refers to Enoch walking with Him. This is the next example where we have the same kind of language about how the Lord walked with Adam and Eve (Genesis 3:8).

In the Garden of Eden the Lord's presence literally was there in a physical form: 'they heard the sound of the LORD God walking in the garden' (Genesis 3:8). Also Cain interacted with the Lord (Genesis 4); when God spoke to Cain after he'd murdered his brother, Cain said, 'and from Your face (presence) I will be hidden' (Genesis 4:14). This appears to be a turning point for Cain, and after this he went away from the Lord's presence. I think it's likely so did his descendants. Why? Because the Bible makes a point of telling us that it was only with the birth of Seth's son that 'at that [same] time men began to call on the name of the LORD' (Genesis 4:26).

Whatever kind of fellowship Enoch had with God, it is evident the Lord wanted to have that closeness with His creation. Though He no longer could walk around enjoying the delights of the garden with those He had created (Genesis 3:8), it didn't stop Him from loving and wanting that level of intimacy with them.

Noah's grandfather, Methuselah, was the longest-living man in the Bible at 969 years old. It is evident that flowing down Noah's generational line was righteousness, and not self-righteousness, because of their reliance on the Lord. Noah didn't earn his righteousness from God because of what he did. Noah was a righteous man because his heart, his character, his inner man, desired to have a constant, unbroken walk with the Lord, and that resulted in right living.

This kind of habitual walk must have built up a sense of trust between Noah and God. Noah knew the Lord's voice; he'd spoken with God many times. And God knew Noah's heart sought after Him. It wasn't like Noah was out one day and God's finger pointed down at him and God said, 'You're the man to build an ark.' Being told by God the earth was about to be destroyed through a flood might have been a shock for Noah, but God speaking to him wasn't.

Favour and grace

Given how Noah walked with the Lord, then, it's not a surprise that we're told how God viewed Noah: 'But Noah found favor *and* grace in the eyes of the LORD' (Genesis 6:8). A sense of favour is mentioned earlier when God respected Abel's offering (Genesis 4:4), but Cain doesn't find any respect in God's eyes when he brings his (Genesis 4:5).[14] And we can read about God's favour many times throughout the Bible. Some examples are:

- Abraham – asked the Lord to stop rather than 'pass by', if he found favour in His eyes (Genesis 18:3);

- David – found favour with the Lord (Acts 7:45-46); and

- Samuel – grew throughout childhood, physically and in the Lord's favour (1 Samuel 2:26).

But when we think of the Lord's favour, what does this mean?

What we mustn't do is confuse God's favour with how we think of it in the worldly sense. It doesn't mean God has favourites, or that we can earn it. When we look at the etymology of the word 'favour', its root stems from the Latin word *favere*; it's about demonstrating affection.[15] God's favour

---

[14] In some Bible translations, such as the NIV UK 2011, the word 'favour' is mentioned in these verses.

[15] For etymology of the word 'favour', see www.etymonline.com/search?q=favere (accessed 10th November 2020).

is part of who He is and how He looks at us. God's favour is all about Him wanting to be kind, wanting to be good to us, and the co-companion of His favour is grace.

If God hadn't told Noah how to build an ark, they wouldn't have known what kind of vessel would be required. It was God's grace towards Noah's family that saved them from the flood's judgement. Remember, it was Noah who 'found favor *and* grace' in God's eyes (Genesis 6:8). We're not told about Emzara, his sons or daughters-in-law's conduct, whether they were righteous or how they behaved. But because Noah was the head of the family, those other seven lives were protected.

When you look at the Genesis 6:8 passage in the Hebrew text, the Hebrew word *ḥên* or *chen* literally means favour and grace.[16] God's grace is echoed many times throughout the Bible, but this is the first time it is explicitly mentioned, whether it's the Hebrew word *ḥên*[17] or English. I wonder whether the first introduction of God's grace coinciding with the ark story is to give us a foretaste of an even more significant act of His grace?

When the angel appeared to Mary many centuries after the flood and said, 'Greetings, favored one' (Luke 1:28), it began the story of grace, and now, with Jesus's death on the cross and resurrection, anyone can be saved:

> For it is by *grace* [God's remarkable compassion and *favor* drawing you to Christ] that you have been saved [actually delivered from judgment and given eternal life] through faith. And this [salvation] is not of yourselves [not through your own effort], but it is the [undeserved, gracious] gift of God.
> (Ephesians 2:8, italics mine)

---

[16] Strong's Hebrew: 2580, Bible Hub, biblehub.com/hebrew/2580.htm (accessed 10th November 2020).

[17] Strong's Hebrew: 2580e, 'Genesis 6:8 Text Analysis,' Hebrew: חֵן (ḥên), English: grace, Bible Hub, biblehub.com/text/genesis/6-8.htm (accessed 10th November 2020).

Because of Jesus, we are living in 'the time of grace' (2 Corinthians 6:2). God's grace doesn't just extend to saving us, it is continual throughout our walk with Him. God's grace wants to bless us abundantly as believers. God looks at us with grace and favour in His eyes. God wants us to be assured of our security in Him because we are the righteousness of God in Jesus (2 Corinthians 5:21).

God's great patience

Though Noah was the only flame flickering in the pre-flood generation of the earth, I think we need to consider the importance of time within this point of the story. What do I mean?

When God spoke to Noah, He could have just snatched him and his family away, like his ancestor Enoch. Enoch didn't die; instead he disappeared; God took him home (Genesis 5:24). But no, God gave Noah time to prepare for the destruction of the earth. Despite the state of the world, God told him to build an ark. This didn't just happen overnight. God didn't say to Noah, 'I'm ending all life and if you look down in the valley, there's a custom-made ark built for you, filled with all the animals and food you'll need.' God gave Noah time.

So by giving Noah time to build and prepare the ark, it meant God had to wait. Peter talks of God's *great* patience' during those days of Noah building the ark (1 Peter 3:20). And we're talking about God who speaks and the world is formed? God who made all of the animals in one day? God who caused the Red Sea to part? It is astounding to think that while the evil continued to escalate, God waited. God waited while one man on the earth, Noah, sawed the planks, measured the door frame, checked the joints, inserted the window, covered the ark with tar. During all of those ark-building and preparation days, God didn't intervene against the evil that caused Him so much pain. God was patient.

Was God waiting to show kindness to everyone else on the earth?

It's clear from the Genesis verses that no one else at that time had the same habitual walk with the Lord as Noah did. But was God waiting in case any of them wanted to be saved? I'd like to think so. I think people could have changed their ways because we know Noah tried to tell them. Noah was a righteous man, and in 2 Peter 2:5 we're told Noah was a 'preacher of righteousness'. A preacher is someone who likes to preach, who likes to speak to people. So I don't think Noah could have stopped himself from talking. I expect Noah spoke to people about God even before he knew about the flood, challenging them to break away from their evil lives. With the news of the earth's imminent destruction, would Noah have stayed silent? I think he would have spoken out even more; unfortunately, no one listened.

Can you imagine the comments that would have been made about him? If they'd had social media back then, I can imagine the posts: #stillNoahbuildsthearkbutnorain. A daily wave of insults and disbelief. A lack of respect that anything Noah shared was credible.

Within this, we mustn't forget Emzara, Tia, Sarah and Mert. They and their husbands didn't hide away for this time. They too must have faced the sarcastic remarks and the growing sense of separation.

Faith

How, then, amid the scale of the practical challenges, threats and scornful contempt from others, did they continue? Well, we know how Noah pressed on; the book of Hebrews tells us the answer – it was:

> By faith [with confidence in God and His word] Noah, being warned *by God* about events not yet seen, in reverence prepared an ark for the salvation of his family. By this [act of obedience] he condemned the world and

became an heir of the righteousness which comes by
faith.
(Hebrews 11:7)

Faith is our enabler. Faith is what activates us to believe in the
things we can't see. It is completely different and distinct from
how we perceive or make judgements in our flesh, in our body.
This verse explains faith even more:

> Now faith is the assurance (title deed, confirmation) of
> *things hoped for (divinely guaranteed)*, and the evidence of
> *things not seen* [the conviction of their reality – faith
> comprehends as fact what cannot be experienced by the
> physical senses].
> (Hebrews 11:1, italics mine)

So thinking of Noah's faith, the 'things hoped for' was the
guarantee God gave to him that he and his family would be
saved from the flood. Then the evidence of 'things not seen'
was the conviction to build an ark for a flood he'd never
experienced.

How could Noah have believed in what God told him if he
didn't have faith? Though Noah had never seen a drop of rain,
though no one else on the earth had either, he 'by faith' knew
he'd have the capability to build the ark, as he worked through
each day shaping the wood with his adze. He 'by faith' believed
the flood would not come until his family could be saved. He
was the only man of his generation to be 'undoubtedly the
subject of unceasing ridicule, but undaunted in his Faith (II
Peter 2:5; Hebrews 11:7)'.[18]

I hope that Noah's family were encouraged by the evidence
of his faith. Whenever Tia, Sarah or Mert saw the ark and
wondered whether what Noah spoke about was real, they would

---

[18] Taken from *Halley's Bible Handbook* by Dr Henry H Halley. Copyright © 1965
by Dr Henry H Halley. Used by permission of Zondervan,
www.zondervan.com, p 73.

have known that day after day he kept diligently working away. Noah was not half-hearted in his obedience, and it was his faith that enabled him to do everything God said.

What can we learn from Noah?

When we reflect on what we've considered about Noah's character, it can make us feel that we wouldn't be able to be like him; that he must have been a man of such great faith. And yes, though we know he had faith, it doesn't mean Noah's faith was the same size as the ark he built. It comes back to how we physically perceive the measure of our faith against what we have faith in.

When I think of my own faith, I can still find myself wanting to rationalise what God has said against how I feel, when often I can't feel anything. It's hard when we live in a world that relies on physical senses. These are often what we rely on to make decisions. We don't cross the road if we see the red stop light. We don't lift a hot dish from the oven with our bare hands. We'll eat up all the cake if it tastes good.

So humanly speaking, it isn't surprising that we want to feel our faith or to see some evidence of it. The assurance of faith though, isn't physical, as it says in the New Living Translation of Hebrews 11:1: 'Faith shows the reality of what we hope for; it is the evidence of things we cannot see.' We can't experience our faith through our senses. We can't feel our faith emotionally. We can't try to have faith through our own doing. Our faith is activated when, 'by faith', we give our lives to Jesus; when we give Him Lordship over our lives and welcome Him as our Saviour and friend. And we continue to demonstrate it through reminding ourselves of God's goodness and the promises in His Word.

Faith doesn't have to be huge. Jesus spoke about faith being like 'the size of a mustard seed' (Matthew 17:20). I've got a mustard seed on my desk as I write this, and they're little, just a couple of millimetres in size, a bit bigger than a full stop.

I love how Jesus knew about mustard seeds, and it was this tiny seed He chose to compare against our faith in Him. This gives me hope. It doesn't matter what size faith Noah had because to Jesus it doesn't matter. Our faith can feel as small as a dot, but if we have that faith we can move mountains in Him. Though circumstances may be tough or challenging, as Noah experienced while building the ark, we can still 'by faith' achieve whatever the Lord tells us to do.

So we might be asking ourselves how we can be like Noah. It is all about our faith, our trust in God. It is because of our faith in what Jesus did that God sees us as righteous and innocent (2 Corinthians 5:21; Ephesians 1:4). Our desire should be to walk in constant habitual fellowship with the Lord, like Noah did, and that's what feeds our faith.

Walking with the Lord is being aware of His presence in our present. We can call on Him any time. And this is something He wants, what His heart wanted when He made us, to spend time together walking around the beautiful garden He'd created. We have to remember, though, while humanity fell and ate the fruit of the tree, God didn't. He doesn't want to be distant from us. He doesn't want to be held at arm's length. His love for us has never changed. He is 'the same yesterday and today and forever' (Hebrews 13:8). Let us be able to say, like Noah, that we walk in a constant relationship with the Lord.[19]

Father, thank You for Your unchanging love and that You look at me with favour and grace. I'm pleasing to You. Thank You for reminding me about faith, and that because of my faith in Jesus, Your Son, You see me as righteous, just as You saw Noah. Help me to learn from Noah's obedience so that, in spite of what others might say around me, I will be faithful to what You speak to me. Whether I feel You with my

---

[19] Author's paraphrase of Genesis 6:9.

*physical senses or not, help me to remember You're always
walking with me, and that by my faith, I walk with You.
Amen.*

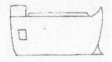

Chapter contemplations

- Consider whether you accept that God looks at you with favour and grace in His eyes. Look up in a concordance scriptures about His love for you. Highlight in your Bible those that stand out to you.

- Meditate on Romans 11:6. Explore in your journal about grace being a gift from God and not based on what we do.

- Make the declaration to be a woman of faith, not fancy, that the substance of your life is founded on your daily walk with the Lord. Remember not to rely on those physical senses!

Journal pages

4

The Flood

Imagine the husbands showing their wives around the ark. Every day the women had seen the ark being built. They walked up a steep ramp leading to the door on the second deck, and once they'd stepped inside, the vast sense of space echoed around them. The sky was just about still visible through the roof being constructed above the third deck. There were ladders and pulleys, levers and planks piled up everywhere. There was a strange smell of pitch in the air as their husbands pointed out where their rooms were and the various areas for the animals. The pots and jars stored near their homes must have looked insignificant compared to the ark's size.

The size of the ark

Though we don't know what their reaction to the ark was like, we do know it was a big boat. God told Noah specifically how to build it. The ark had to be 300 cubits long, fifty cubits wide and thirty cubits high (Genesis 6:15). When we translate the measurements into those we have today, we can fully comprehend the ark's scale. This means the ark was 510ft or 155m long and 50ft or 15m high. In other terms, the length of the ark could be filled with one and a half football fields or three space shuttles laid out end to end, and the ark's height was taller than a four-storey house.[20] When you think of how many animals and how much food could be stored, the Ark Encounter helpfully compares the ark to having 'enough capacity to hold at least 120,000 sheep'.[21] I like sheep, but that's a lot! Though there wouldn't have been that many sheep on the ark, it makes us realise how many actual animals could be accommodated.

The world in which the women lived would not have been able to ignore the ark. There wasn't anything else for its size to contend with. No high-rise blocks of flats or grand skyscrapers in those times. Yet as the ark loomed higher and higher, and larger and larger within its landscape, people ignored it. For them, normal day-to-day life continued regardless of this crazy man still going on about building the ark and warning them of the impending flood.

All the days the ark continued to be built, the women knew they had time to prepare. How could the world flood if the ark wasn't ready? Picture Tia as she lingered over what precious items to take in her carved trunk, Sarah selecting all the strands of thread for the wall coverings she planned to sew, Mert dithering about how many belts to pack. Yet, as the last planks of the roof were hammered into place, as the inside of the third deck was coated with pitch, that feeling of haste must have increased. Though they didn't know when the flood would start, the sign of the ark in front of them was nearing completion.

How long did it take to build the ark?

The Bible doesn't give us any indication as to how long it took Noah to build the ark, or how long it stood ready until eight human lives and all the animals went into it. We're told in Genesis 5:32 that Noah was 500 years old when he had his sons.

---

[20] 'How Big Was Noah's Ark?' Ark Encounter, arkencounter.com/noahs-ark/size/ (accessed 2nd November 2020). Permission given from Answers in Genesis. The Ark Encounter is a life-sized ark in Kentucky, USA.
[21] Ibid. Permission given from Answers in Genesis.

God refers to Noah's sons and their wives when He tells him about the flood (Genesis 6:18). We also know from Genesis 7:6 that Noah was 600 years old when the deluge started. So we can glean a 100-year time period from those two verses. During that time, Japheth, Shem and Ham had to reach an age when they could marry, and then at some point within this God told Noah about the flood. There are other viewpoints about whether the 120 years mentioned in Genesis 6:3 is the length of time God gave Noah, but this is not conclusive. We've already spoken about God's great patience through the ark-building time, so from this, and from what we can understand from the Scriptures, I think there were years of pre-flood preparations, not days.

With the ark now completed, Noah and his family must have wondered if the flood was imminent. However, even with the ark standing ready, still they didn't know. Why? Because though God had told Noah he and his family were going to enter the ark, God didn't tell Noah *when* He was going to tell them to go aboard. We don't know how long God waited after the ark was ready before He spoke.

So this meant they had to carry on with their daily activities, continue to prepare, and perhaps as Emzara and the other women packed the harvest of apples into wooden boxes, they thought this might actually be the last time they'd do it.

Seven days

Then came the time they were waiting for. God spoke to Noah: 'In seven days I am going to cause it to rain on the earth for forty days and forty nights' (Genesis 7:4). With this news came the countdown to the destruction of lives around them. The flood was imminent. Though they had spent years preparing for it, now it became even more of a reality.

If Emzara walked around the village, did she look at the people bustling in the market thinking they had only seven days to live? Noah must have preached with even greater intensity, 'The flood is coming in seven days. Turn to God, save yourself.'

But did the once-friends-now-strangers splutter into their drinks and turn their backs, laughing? They'd heard it all before.

Though the Lord's words gave Noah and the family another layer of confirmation to know the flood was going to happen soon, they still had to trust. They still had to believe that in seven days this strange, unfathomable thing called rain would fall. Remember, they only knew it was seven days. God didn't tell Noah exactly at what hour, minute or second the first drop of rain would fall. Those seven days for the women must have created such a mixture of emotions, wanting the flood to come so they could get on the ark and make a start with whatever that would bring, but then a sense of disbelief that the world was going to change. Did they spend their time trying to remember every detail, or did they earnestly focus on their preparations?

I think it's interesting that God gave them the time warning so they could prepare. Practically, this meant everything they did wasn't hypothetical – the boxes of apples they'd packed would be needed. They could truly load everything onto the ark, knowing it was soon going to become their home. I also think the time warning of seven days reinforces the kindness of God's heart so they didn't have to wait until the first drop of rain fell on their heads to know the flood had started. Can you imagine the kind of panic this would have caused them?

My interpretation is, though they had the seven days to prepare, it wasn't until the seventh day that they entered the ark, as it states here:

> On the very same day Noah and Shem and Ham and Japheth, the sons of Noah, and Noah's wife and the three wives of his sons with them, entered the ark.
> (Genesis 7:13)

Along with them entered all the animals. But I'm jumping ahead of myself here. Let's return to the seven days' warning God gave Noah. Doesn't that seem familiar? Isn't it how the Lord speaks to us? Sometimes we can feel in our spirits that something is going to happen; we may get a timescale, but more often than not we have a sense of soon.

The sense of soon

Before you say, 'Aren't we talking about physical senses here?' I want to clarify – no. This *sense of soon* is a prompting from the Holy Spirit. We believe our God is three-in-one: Father, Jesus His Son, and the Holy Spirit. The Holy Spirit is important in our lives; we're filled with the Holy Spirit when we believe in Jesus. He is the connection with our spirit. He gives us discernment.

For a couple of years I travelled to Heathrow each autumn for work events. Each time I left Heathrow's tube station to the sound of planes taking off and landing every thirty seconds, I just knew in my spirit I would be taking off in a plane from Heathrow to go to America... soon.

'That's obvious,' I hear you say. 'You can go across the pond any time to go on holiday.' True, I had a passport, but I hadn't ventured outside the UK since I'd left America as a very young child in difficult circumstances. My home commitments meant I wouldn't have considered making such a trip. So though it's something I could have done, for me it wasn't a reality at that time. Yet I have a very distinct memory of sitting in the hotel dining room eating my breakfast and knowing it would happen. I would be returning to America and meeting family I'd never seen.

Of course, I didn't stay there in the hotel and wait until it happened; I had an event to lead. But the *sense of soon* I felt in my spirit filled me with hope and expectation, that despite my reality, which seemed impossible and unreal, I knew it would occur. I had to wait more than seven days, though, for God to turn the knowing into going.

In autumn 2018, three years since I had first sensed the whisper of soon in my spirit, I was again at Heathrow, this time heading to the airport along with my mum and two large suitcases – we were flying to America. It hadn't been an easy time up until that point, with unforeseen changes and personal loss I wouldn't have imagined. But as we drove around the familiar roundabout at Heathrow (the one with the big plane on it, if you know the area), I praised the Lord. He alone knew the timings.

Since I first felt that *sense of soon*, I had to wait and have faith. I had to trust and leave it in His hands; it wasn't something I could make happen. It was the Lord who knew about the combination of events which would lead up to that moment, and I had to be obedient and continue to listen to Him.

The suddenly

Day six turned into day seven and Noah and his family woke for the last time in their homes. The *sense of soon* must have felt even closer. This was still the pre-flood earth which had the Garden of Eden with the cherubim and the sword's 'flashing blade' to stop people from entering (Genesis 3:24). The same earth where Nephilim roamed (Genesis 6:4).

People woke up and got on with their lives, thinking about what they'd do tomorrow. The farmers checked on their crops. The blacksmiths forged iron. There were weddings and parties, people bustling around eating and drinking, listening to music, enjoying the celebrations. Rain interrupted them.

At a time only known by God on that seventh day, first one raindrop fell from the sky, then another, and another, and another... until you couldn't see through the torrents pouring down. The sky was no longer a brilliant blue, but had become a grey, cloudy mass. The sun had cast its last shadow for a while:

> In the six hundredth year of Noah's life, on the seventeenth day of the second month, on that same day all the fountains of the great deep [subterranean waters] burst open, and the windows *and* floodgates of the heavens were opened.
> (Genesis 7:11)

There were Noah, his sons and their wives going into the ark, the animals scuttling, scurrying and sliding up the ramp. *Suddenly* water lashed against the ark. *Suddenly* there was no other safety except in the salvation of it. *Suddenly* for the first time Emzara felt the sensation of rain on her face.

Would they have been scared? You'd expect it, wouldn't you? It feels like something which would happen in a movie; something dreamt up by a Hollywood screenwriter. The thought of rain to them was as unreal to us that in 2020 a virus would lead to a pandemic across the globe.

I think the world outside the ark would have been very afraid. People would have been trying and failing to save themselves in any way possible. I wonder if Emzara looked out of the ark's door waiting for someone to run out of the village? Or did the sudden volume of water sweep people away?

We know from natural disasters, or if our own homes have been flooded, how quickly water levels can change, and the damage that can be done within a very short period of time. Water has incredible strength, weight and power. On that seventh day the entire pre-flood earth experienced the devastation water can bring.

When did the flood take place?

When we think of planet Earth and how long it has existed, we may be accustomed to its age being in the millions or billions of years. We hear these kinds of numbers in the media, we learn about evolution in education, theories have become fact and this kind of language has become commonplace in how history is related.

The Bible doesn't tell us that the flood happened in year X, but experts have used chronological information to calculate a date, just as we can biblically date the age of the earth. This information places the flood at around '2304 BC ± 11 years'.[22] I

[22] Dr John Osgood, 'The Date of Noah's Flood', Creation Ministries International, online article sourced from *Creation* magazine, Volume 4, Issue 1,

realise some of you reading this may be sceptical, or think, 'Why should I believe this just because you say so?' There are some very good sources[23] available, so I'd suggest you explore these, because there is archaeological and scientific evidence which gives credibility to the flood and that it wasn't billions of years ago.

God closes the ark's door

Noah and his family entered the ark continuing to not know, but still go. They didn't know how long the flood would last, how much time they would spend on the ark or what was going to happen to the earth. For the last time they looked out on the rain-soaked world they knew, and God closed the ark's door (Genesis 7:16).

Yes, you don't need to reread that. God closed the ark's door. Why did He do this?

I think God closed the door because He wanted to demonstrate His protection. The ark was a man-made structure. Remember, God didn't pre-order a ready-made version and deliver it to Noah. Though human hands had built the ark, God was gracious to give them a sign at a moment in time when they must have been frightened, must have wondered if they'd be safe. God showed His love and authority as the door slammed shut behind them, through no human effort. He was showing them He would continue to keep them safe. He would not fail in His promises made to Noah.

When the rain suddenly started, it was the culmination of the words God had spoken to Noah years before. The ark had been built, food stored and collected and they'd waited for this day. Some of those questions they'd had right back at the start had been answered. But now the family faced more uncertainty,

March 1981, pp 10-13, creation.com/the-date-of-noahs-flood (accessed 2nd November 2020). Permission given from Creation Ministries International.
[23] Such as Answers in Genesis, answersingenesis.org (accessed 2nd November 2020) and Creation Ministries International, creation.com (accessed 2nd November 2020).

more waiting in this greater unknown until it was safe enough for the ark's door to be opened again.

Suddenlies and safety

Though they'd had some warning and the women knew the rain was coming, the suddenness of it still must have taken them by surprise; the shock as they saw the beginning of the end for the pre-flood earth. The ark was their only safe refuge and they must have welcomed its protection.

We talk about shelter in a storm. We wear the necessary clothes and shoes when we go for a hike. We put on sun cream to protect our skin from its damaging rays.

In the suddenlies of our lives, we often don't have the chance to prepare. As with the unexpected and unfamiliar, the suddenly comes out of nowhere and we can be shaken. We're afraid. So many thoughts cross our minds as we try to process the situation, to plan what we need to do, when actually all we might want to do is run away and hide, to find that protection.

Some suddenlies can be good, like winning a competition, and I'm sure you can think of others. But whether the suddenly is what we consider to be good or bad, both have a common theme. They require some form of action.

We may think of resilience at this point. The word has a connection to how well we manage what the world throws at us. How well we can bounce back. We hear the stories about people's fortitude through adversity and can admire their inner strength. We can read books that give us tools to use. Yet these give us another expectation about how we should be. And though we might try to learn how to manage some circumstances, to be more resilient, in the times of the suddenly, when we're afraid, when we don't know what to do, however much resilience *we* think *we've* got, it can run away in the opposite direction.

Sometimes I go for a walk along a tree-lined path that leads to a lake in Arundel, a town close to where I live. As well as the canopy of branches above me, when I look up to the left, I see the massive structure of a medieval castle. I've walked there through the seasons, and I notice something different each time, but I always find myself standing and staring at the castle's tower, thinking about how it is still intact despite everything that has happened throughout history. I'm also reminded as I look that 'The name of the LORD is a strong tower' (Proverbs 18:10). In that moment I'm making the comparison about how the tower is like what the Lord represents. But the actual Proverbs verb isn't a comparison. When we read it closely, the verse isn't saying the Lord's name is *like a tower*. No, the verse says the Lord's name *'is* a strong tower' (italics mine).

Into the suddenly of the rain came the safety of the ark. Into our suddenly comes the safety of the Lord. When we're afraid, when we have no idea, when we have no fortitude or resilience, we can go to the One who does. And where does the safety come from? His name: 'The righteous runs to it and is safe *and* set on high' (Proverbs 18:10). In the strength of Jesus' name, we'll find our own strength increasing and our fears decreasing as we enter into His protection.

As Noah and his family stood in the ark, the rain lashing outside, there was no other choice than to take shelter in its protection. The next step of their unknown journey had begun.

Father, thank You that nothing is a surprise to You, from the day the first drop of rain fell on the earth to what I'm experiencing in my life now as I've read this chapter. Thank You for the encouragement we read about in the Genesis verses, that You are true to Your promises. What You first spoke of to Noah did happen, but You kept them safe. The ark was their refuge. Help me to remember, when I encounter the suddenlies in my life, that You've given me safety too in Your name. Give me the hope of a soon in my heart, or if I'm waiting on one, then help me to continue to trust in You for Your timings.
Amen.

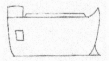

Chapter contemplations

- Consider times where you've felt a *sense of soon* in your spirit. How did you identify that what you sensed was from the Lord and not your own desires? Spend some time writing your thoughts in your journal.

- Share with a friend about how you've faced your own suddenlies.

- Read Psalm 32, paying particular attention to verse 7.

Journal pages

5
Sound of Rain

The door had slammed shut on the ark. The world decreased from the macro to the micro. As the women made their way through the ark's corridors, a cacophony of different sights and smells were all around them. The bellows of unfamiliar animals. The call of birds. Along with the incessant rhythm of rain.

There were the practicalities of settling the animals in, feeding them, preparing a meal for the family and getting used to where everything was. This time it wasn't a visit; this time the ark was their home. Imagine the flood of emotions going through the women's minds: grief, fear, shock, relief, tiredness, awe...

Picture Emzara as she tossed and turned on the first night: Noah was fast asleep, but all she could hear was the rain drumming against the ark. Though she covered her ears, the sound pounded inside her head. Here they were all safe from its judgement, but the rain's beat reminded her of the immense loss of life outside; what she should have done about it. She feels scared that she doesn't like the sound of rain. She shouldn't feel like that; she's Mrs Noah.

The word 'should'

Whether we say the word aloud or internally, when we use the word 'should' as a form of self-criticism, it usually brings along a friend, and that friend is a feeling.

How does the word make you feel? Maybe you've even thought that you *should* be doing something else rather than reading this page?

When I hear 'should', it makes me feel like there is a judge pointing a finger at me. And I find myself not meeting the measure of what the word tells me and wonder what I should be doing to get there.

Martha comes to mind at this point. Jesus goes into her home for a meal with all His disciples. We're not told whether this is a surprise or a planned visit, but we do know from reading Luke 10:38-42 that Martha likes to be busy, working away thinking of everything she should be doing for the meal. So there she is, one job completed, on to the next, then she mustn't forget the thing to do after that. And in the midst of ticking off all the should-bes for herself, she even has time to think about a should for her sister. Mary shouldn't be sitting at Jesus' feet.

While Jesus speaks to Mary, He's not ignorant of everything Martha's doing, and when Martha comes up to Jesus, she's essentially asking Him to 'Tell my sister she should be helping me!'

Listen to how Jesus responds: 'Martha, Martha, you are worried and bothered *and* anxious about so many things' (Luke 10:41).

Jesus doesn't do what Martha asks; instead, He acknowledges how she feels. He calls out the feelings created by the should-be: *worry*, *bother*, *anxiety*. These are fuelling all of Martha's busyness. Hands up, I have those emotions many times. Do I identify them, call them out for what they are? Sometimes. Do I more often than not entertain them? Yes.

I work myself up into the tortuous never-ending cycle of bothering over worries or work I've anxiously engendered from the should-be. It sounds exhausting even writing this. But that state of mind is so all-consuming and wearying. Although once voiced the word 'should' quickly disappears, its friends want to stay around a lot longer.

When we listen to the should

If we listen to the should-bes of life, then are we living? Are we able to centre on what is happening around us without discombobulating ourselves because of what should be? And can we really enjoy the moment we're in if we're always thinking about something else we should be doing?

Yes, we may need to get certain jobs done. We may want to feel a certain way, but listening to should makes us doubt ourselves. We become detracted from what we're doing, or from our current emotional state, through imposing this self-judgement about how else we should be investing our time or emotions. If we do listen and agree and switch to whatever should dictates, then does it reward us?

Instead there is a drip, drip, drip effect with this form of internal analysis. Once we turn on the tap and allow ourselves to think in this way, then we very quickly find those not-so-friendly feelings pouring out. We seek ways to back up what we're thinking and may even find ourselves wanting to qualify them. We know we shouldn't be thinking this way about ourselves, but rather than stopping, we make it worse by adding, 'I shouldn't feel like that. I'm a mum, wife, friend, believer…'

Though it might have been a simple should that appeared in our thoughts, once we entertain it, then we enter into a state of negative self-evaluation. It's harder to not find even more confirmation about our thoughts, so we take on board the feelings that arise from looking at social media or comments made to us by others. Everything seems to confirm our apparent failures. The water gushes over.

It's all about the associations we make of the word 'should'. What do I mean?

Well, we can't not listen to it. Once we've thought or used the word in context to ourselves, we're not able to forget what we've heard. The sound of rain had no pleasing associations for Noah and his family. They wouldn't have heard the rain's pitter-patter against a tent's canvas roof or experienced the refreshing coolness of a shower on a scorching summer's day. It's the same with any form of self-criticism. When we have those internal triggers, we find it harder to ignore them. The emotional associations want to stay around and claim our attention.

Why we listen to the should

When we drop a plate on the floor we might tut and think, 'Silly me!' But listening to the shoulds we say and think is more than scolding ourselves.

Could we say we want to listen to the worry and anxiety behind the should, even though we know those emotions can numb us from the now or deaden our decisions?

Worrying can be very appealing. I know that myself. If we have a propensity to feel worried and anxious, then listening to should opens the door, and we can easily enter into a conversation without realising it. One word results in us listening to many more. We find ourselves embroiled with all those thoughts consuming us.

At first, worrying seems OK; surely it's part of being cautious, of thinking about what might happen? But it overtakes us, and we find ourselves unable to stop, but yet strangely we also feel like we don't want to.

Why is worrying like that?

When we're worrying, it's like we're running our bodies at a high state. Think of keeping the car engine revving. We get used to it. We pick worry up, just like when we automatically check our phone as soon as we wake up. You see, whether our words are spoken, thought or written, they are powerful. Words are extremely seductive:

> Death and life are in the power of the tongue,
> And those who love it *and* indulge it will eat its fruit and
> bear the consequences of their words.
> (Proverbs 18:21)

We often think of this verse in regard to the words we speak, and that's true. But it also applies to what we say internally. We bear the consequences of our own words. The weight of all those worrying thoughts is strong and oppressive, 'Worry weighs us down' (Proverbs 12:25, *The Message*). It cripples us internally and manifests itself physically. We become consumed by it and find ourselves struggling to find a way out. We panic. We don't feel well. We feel condemned because we shouldn't be so stupid as to be worrying in the first place.

Though we may find some relief in following coping strategies and other worldly advice, still those feelings linger; like a shadow, they follow us around. We try to block them out because we know what's going to happen as soon as we enter into the conversation. We worry about not worrying.

I'd like to think Paul wrote this passage in Philippians from what he had learned in his relationship with God. We know it isn't as simple as saying to ourselves, 'Don't fret or worry.' We're just not wired that way; we have emotions. I think the apostle Paul had learned what do to with his worry:

> Don't fret or worry. Instead of worrying, pray. Let petitions and praises *shape* your worries into prayers, letting God know your concerns. Before you know it, a sense of God's wholeness, everything coming together for good, will come and settle you down. It's wonderful what happens when Christ displaces worry at the center of your life.
> (Philippians 4:6-7, *The Message*, italics mine)

So what Paul's saying here is that there's a way out of worry: 'Instead ... pray.'

How do we pray?

We're praising God, telling Him about all those worries He already knows about. I love how *The Message* translation uses the verb 'shape' in relation to the petitions and praises we make in our prayers. That shows change. Think of when we have to shape something, such as making cake decorations. We take a block of fondant icing and mould it. That's what I think Paul means here, that through prayer we're shaping the heavy weight of raw feelings… there's a process. And crucially, while we pray, we're also praising. Why praise?

Because as we begin to share our feelings with God and call on Him, we're kneading and sculpting those raw emotions. But we're still focused on them; we're only looking at the icing. Yet as our language turns into praise it engages our spirit; it pulls on the connection we have with the Holy Spirit in us. As we acknowledge God's greatness, our worry shifts. And look what Paul learned: as we do that, before we're even aware, the emotions will dissipate. It doesn't mean everything causing those feelings and fears, all those *shoulds*, will disappear, but it's like Jesus has come alongside us and given us a chance to breathe. Out of the heaviness, out of the lump of fondant icing, a flower appears; something good comes. His wholeness reassures us.

The difference between should and could

Sometimes what prompts us to speak or think this way can be out of our control – a circumstance or situation we didn't expect to encounter – and we try to process how we're now going to work through this thing… whatever that thing is. Words start to materialise. We won't use the word 'should' all the time, but when we do it can often take us by surprise.

As I'm writing this sentence, I'm sat at my desk, and I catch sight of a big pile of paperwork; unprompted comes the thought, 'I *should* be getting on with that.' I then feel worried because I know I need to action some letters, but how am I going to get that done when I need to finish the chapter? None of this was going through my thoughts before should entered. What do I do now?

I have a straightforward literal choice. I could either continue writing, or I could close my laptop and reach for the papers.

I have a harder emotional choice, because now I'm feeling worried about everything I have to do and how much the time is ticking away. Then I start to feel anxious about an email I sent this morning, and before I know it I'm feeling swamped.

So, do we have a choice?

Yes, there is a difference between should and could. What we need to do is differentiate and ask whether the *should* needs to be acted upon or whether we *could* choose not to. We have the choice to swat should away. Sometimes that might be, 'Yes, I could be doing the paperwork instead, but I'm choosing to write.' It could be not dwelling too much on social media posts where we feel we should be doing what everyone else is doing; we have a choice to stop scrolling through on our mobiles. And if our emotional state is one way, and we think it should be another, then thinking *could* instead means we're recognising our emotions – we could be and we may indeed feel that way, but not at the moment.

So how could we be?

We've talked about how the word 'should' introduces self-criticism and opens us up to worry and anxiety. We become introspective and judge ourselves: 'The first to speak in court sounds right – until the cross-examination begins' (Proverbs 18:17, NLT). So it's easy to believe our feelings, to think that our self-assessment is right. But if Jesus were to stand up and cross examine our feelings, what would He say?

The reality is, we are going to get worried or anxious. Though we have the choice to not listen to the should, though we can swat it away sometimes, we may still find ourselves struggling. Jesus didn't tell Martha off because of how she felt, neither did He say the shoulds that Martha thought were right. He didn't agree that Mary should help her sister. Instead He said:

> ... but *only* one thing is necessary, for Mary has chosen the good part [that which is to her advantage], which will not be taken away from her.
> (Luke 10:42)

What is 'the good part'? What was Mary doing?

She chose to listen to the words Jesus was speaking, unlike Martha who was focused on all those internal thoughts about what she should have been doing. See, 'the good part' is listening to the words Jesus says, the life and truth in them, because that is who He is (John 14:6).

There is another aspect to the sound of rain which Emzara wasn't aware of on the ark – life. Rain renews, refreshes, restores. Without rain, nothing would grow. And Jesus speaks the edifying, life-giving, love-filled words we need to hear.

So if Jesus were to cross-examine our self-judgements, I think He'd call them out. I don't think He'd agree with those emotions – the weight and burden of them. I don't think He'd want us entering into a worry-filled state of mind. I don't think He'd like us talking about ourselves like that because He doesn't speak that way about us. 'For the word of the LORD is right' (Psalm 33:4) and we are 'precious' to Him (Isaiah 43:4).

When we are in the maelstrom of our should storm, whatever its cause, when we can't switch off the sound of the rain, we need to remind ourselves about who we are in Him. And even if in the weight of the worry we can't speak the words of life to ourselves, we praise Him. We let Him shape those worries. We remind ourselves who He says we are. Otherwise those harsh words and emotions will rob and destroy us.

On the ark it was day three, and outside the weather roared. Emzara had not been able to ignore the rain and the worrying continued. Her cry could have echoed with David's 'I'm desperate for a change from rage and stormy weather' (Psalm 55:8, *The Message*). Maybe Noah noticed Emzara's anxious state and gently reminded her that God had told him before they entered that the rain was only going to last 'for forty days and forty nights' (Genesis 7:4). Aboard the ark, the sound of rain would eventually come to an end.

For us, rain will fall. We can't control when the should-be clouds fill our thoughts. But we can release and pour out the pressure that builds from those emotions. We can choose not to busy ourselves with the *should* – we can think *could*. We can cast aside those unfriendly emotions to the best friend we have, placing:

> [all your anxieties, all your worries, and all your concerns, once and for all] on Him, for He cares about you [with deepest affection, and watches over you very carefully].
> (1 Peter 5:7)

Father, it is so easy to speak and say words without realising what I'm actually saying to myself, or how those words make me feel inside. Though I might judge myself, I'm so glad You don't. Thank You that You want to help me when I'm overcome with worry; when I can't stop myself from being in this state of mind. When I'm overwhelmed, thank You that You alone give me a way out. When I'm caught up in the busyness or emotions created by what I think I should be doing, remind me of Your life-affirming words. I've chosen life in You and You are constantly declaring life over me. You're singing over me.[24] All praise and honour to You.
Amen.

---

[24] Zephaniah 3:17, NKJV.

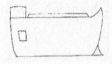

Chapter contemplations

- Identify and be conscious over the next couple of days of any self-critical words you think or say about yourself. Is there a pattern? Spend some time reflecting with your journal and Jesus.

- Remember, you have a choice. When someone says to you *should* or you say the word to yourself, give those feelings that accompany it to Jesus, and don't let yourself be led down the should-be path.

- Make a list or highlight Bible verses about God's goodness – start with Psalm 34. When you bring those worries to Him, these will help you to shape your prayers and bring the power of His life-giving words.

Journal pages

6

The Want in the Wait

We might initially think the Noah's ark story is all about the family and animals entering the ark, the rain falling, and then them all leaving and seeing the rainbow. It gives us an impression that they weren't on the ark for very long, when actually there was a very long period of waiting for all the animals and the eight people before they could leave.

Forty days and nights of rain

The rainy days have continued. In some countries there are monsoon seasons, periods when it just doesn't stop raining for days on end, but these are places where people are accustomed to the rain. We know from the previous chapter that the sound of rain was a new experience for everyone aboard the ark, as was living together with a multitude of animals. Think about what those early days might have been filled with: discovering new creatures, settling into routines, learning to live with each other, and getting used to living within the confines of a large vessel, each day and night being accompanied by the never-ending rain.

Day thirty-nine turned into day forty. Did they think they would be able to leave after the fortieth day? Was that their expectation? The rain continued to pour incessantly. Then, when they woke on the forty-first day, there was a change. God had kept His promise – the rain ceased after the fortieth night.

However, there was no way they were going to be able to leave the ark. Because there was another noise: the sound of the floodwaters moving underneath them. The rain's persistent beat had been replaced with a swaying motion. The ark was fully afloat:

> The flood [the great downpour of rain] was forty days *and* nights on the earth; and the waters increased and lifted up the ark, and it floated [high] above the land. The waters became mighty and increased greatly on the earth, and the ark floated on the surface of the waters. The waters prevailed so greatly *and* were so mighty *and* overwhelming on the earth, so that all the high mountains everywhere under the heavens were covered. [In fact] the waters became fifteen cubits higher [than the highest ground], and the mountains were covered. All living beings that moved on the earth perished – birds and cattle (domestic animals), [wild] animals, all things that swarm *and* crawl on the earth, and all mankind. Everything on the dry land, all in whose nostrils was the breath *and* spirit of life, died.
> (Genesis 7:17-22)

Imagine the world covered with floodwaters and the ark floating over the top of them with just eight people and the animals inside. The only living creatures outside were those who lived in the sea. Remember it says, 'Everything on the dry land … died'. Noah didn't need to build an aquarium compartment for the blue whale.

When the ark floated, the women must have realised their time on the ark would continue. The rain stopping wasn't the end of their journey. I think this must have given them mixed feelings. I wonder whether they understood that now, with this volume of water, nothing on the earth had survived (Genesis 7:21)? As they walked around the ark, trying not to bump into the walls, trying to get used to the motion, did they try not to think about everything that had been left behind?

Along with this awareness must have come the reality that they were stuck on the ark. Other than the warning about when the flood would start and how long the rain would last (Genesis 7:4), God hadn't given Noah any other timing information. They knew they would be kept alive (Genesis 6:18), but how long would they need to wait? All they could do was hope in what lay ahead, but what would that be? More questions, with nothing to divert their attention. As the initial feelings wore off, the women couldn't escape from the surroundings of the ark's wooden walls. All they could do was wait.

All we can do is wait

That's easy to say, isn't it? However, waiting is one of the hardest things to do. In the pace of our modern lives, we can get what we want, when we want it – if we have the resources to be able to do so. Waiting when we've made a choice, though, is very different from enforced waiting. What do I mean by this?

Well, the women on the ark didn't have a choice. They had to wait. The ark was their safety against the waters surrounding them. With the worldwide pandemic, everyone across the globe in one way or another had to wait because of the enforcements. Unexpectedly, we were placed in a form of constraint to protect lives. Though each country used its own measures, all of us had to get used to not having the freedom to do what we wanted; to have to wait to see loved ones, go to a coffee shop, have a holiday, even wait to be able to leave our homes. It felt surreal.

If someone had told me a year earlier that I would have to stay indoors, that I would only be able to go out once a day for exercise and essential shopping, that I would not be able to see anyone other than those living with me, I would have thought it was crazy.

At the time of writing, the UK was preparing to enter its second lockdown. The life we experienced in 2019 and before hadn't returned, and we didn't know if it would. We had to wait for a solution, be that a vaccine or something else. Could we adapt? How would we handle it? Each one of us has our own experiences about the challenges and difficulties we faced during this time.

Living in lockdown or circuit breakers gave us a taste of what it must have felt like for the women on the ark. We were told our homes were our safe space. Some people had to get used to working from home; home-schooling their children. For others who were furloughed from their jobs, there was the apparent luxury of free time.

Before I left my job in London, I craved time. I think when we're busy, time is in high demand. We always need to get things done. With twelve-hour days, often longer when the commute got delayed, and packed weekends, I thought when I left I'd be able to catch up on things. I was wrong! I've learned over the last couple of years that life continues to throw things at us. Whatever our circumstances, time is difficult to manage and there is never enough.

During the lockdown, I was aware of a lot of social media content that could have made us feel bad if we didn't do certain things with all this apparent *free time*. For parents balancing working from home and looking after their children, there wasn't the luxury of being able to tackle projects. For others, the sheer emotional shock of the situation made it hard to just go through each day. For some, their working life continued. Yet everyone, irrespective of their circumstances, was waiting for this time period to be over. It's strange how, even while we're waiting, there's an expectation that we need to get on with things, for others to tell us what we *should* be doing.

Enforced waiting like this is hard. We can't do what we usually would to handle the emotions that arise when we're under pressure.

Think of the ark – if Tia usually went for a walk in the fields when she was stressed, then all she would have been able to do was walk around the enclosed corridors when she needed some space, but this wasn't the same as being outside or necessarily what she wanted.

That's the thing with waiting – we can't do what we want, and this creates a struggle with self.

The difference between want and wait

There is always going to be some kind of *want in the wait*. It might be what others want us to do, or our own desires. Let's just think a moment, though, about what the words mean.

- *Want* centres around what we require, and the word's root comes from an Old Norse word which is about lack.

- *Wait* is about time passing, usually while we're still in the same place. Its root goes back to being attentive.[25]

We have many different wants and waits, don't we? The small kind of want: I'm thirsty, which is immediately satisfied when we have a drink; to the larger: I want a house, I want to know where I'm going. I want to be married, I want my life to change… Though what we think we want may not always be what we need. To us it feels like it's something we lack, something we believe will make our lives better.

Then there are the different waits. Waiting for the water to come to the boil so we can make a hot drink. Waiting for the test result from the doctor. Waiting for answers to some of those big 'want' questions which don't get answered quickly, or may not be answered at all.

Still on the ark, still waiting

Noah, his family and all the animals waited while the ark rocked. Two months became three…

---

[25] For etymology of the words 'want' and 'wait' see
www.etymonline.com/search?q=want and
www.etymonline.com/search?q=wait (accessed 5th November 2020).

The initial excitement and challenge of new things had worn off. The women had settled into their new routines and with this ease, and the passing of time, their different personality traits and characteristics pushed and pulled together. Like with any period of waiting, I think they must have experienced expectations, frustrations and irritations on the ark. What do I mean?

Expectations

When we're in a season of waiting, it's natural to expect it to end, even if we don't have anyone conclusively confirming an end date to us. But is it unrealistic to have this expectation? At some point Emzara must have expected she'd be leaving the ark.

Often people will talk about managing our expectations so that we don't build up our thoughts and end up disappointing ourselves. Do we feel bad about having expectations while we wait? Can believers have expectations?

Well, David knew about waiting when he wrote Psalm 27. He describes how to wait, and with expectation too:

> *I would have despaired* had I not believed that I would see
> the goodness of the LORD
> In the land of the living.
> Wait for *and* confidently expect the LORD;
> Be strong and let your heart take courage;
> Yes, wait for *and* confidently expect the LORD.
> (Psalm 27:13-14)

David realised he needed hope, he needed something to expect, something to believe in, otherwise he 'would have despaired'. There is a correlation between hope, belief and expectations, but the key for believers is whom we place our expectations in. So where does David's advice lead?

To the Lord.

Notice how David describes expecting, though. He says, '*confidently* expect the LORD' (v14, italics mine). Though I'm not in employment at the moment, I'm expecting to find work, even though I don't know what that will be in the climate of increased unemployment and economic uncertainty. I can be confident, though, not because I'm convinced in my own abilities but because I believe in the goodness of Jesus to provide (Philippians 4:19).

It doesn't mean we're not going to lose hope or feel like we are, it doesn't mean we aren't going to be challenged while we wait, or that everything we're expecting will happen. But it's about reminding ourselves of the Father's heart for us. It's the choice we make to believe in His goodness, to grip hold of that courage and expectantly wait for Him, knowing that He does have a good plan for us (Jeremiah 29:11). This is the unseen element of faith we have working within us. This isn't about placing our expectations on sinking sand, but on the strong foundation we have in Him (Matthew 7:24-27).

Frustrations

This is when we can't do what our will wants.

For me during the first lockdown, I found it very frustrating not being able to go to the coffee shop. With hindsight, I can see it was probably not a great habit, but I was used to getting my soya-extra-hot-latte-with-sugar-free-gingerbread-syrup. It was something I found comforting. I wanted it, but I couldn't have it. It was hard in those first lockdown days; I missed it. You'll be pleased to hear I didn't end up stomping my feet like a toddler, and I got used to enjoying the delights of having coffee at home. Though this example may sound simple, it can often be the simpler things that frustrate us when we wait.

What can be especially annoying is when *something* happens while we're waiting which gets us excited; we can feel that change coming. But the *something* is only a chink, which makes us feel encouraged but it doesn't completely satisfy. It reinforces how hard it is to keep waiting. Our will demands something to happen faster.

In our frustration we start to attempt to force and push things, to go against advice. We saw the increase of people becoming exasperated with the pandemic; it stirred up many levels of frustration and anger. A lot of countries had an increase in virus numbers because people were annoyed with their government's restrictions and how they implemented policies. In their desires of self, people went against the rules in place. Though they may have known at one level they shouldn't do something, their own self-will's internal message was stronger.

So, can we wait and not be frustrated?

Humanly, I think it's impossible. Frustration is one of those emotions we all have; it's a natural response, but again it's another one of those emotions that can overtake us. Frustration can deepen into anger and a very determined feeling.

What about submission? How does that link to frustration? Well, isn't that what we do? We either *submit to our will* and do what we want regardless, or we *bring our will into submission* and don't follow what it seeks. Therefore, would bringing our will into submission stop our frustrations from controlling us?

The thing I hear you say is, 'We're not going to be able to submit to ourselves – our will does what it wants.' Exactly! *The Message* translation explains it well:

> My counsel is this: Live freely, animated and motivated by God's Spirit. Then you won't feed the compulsions of selfishness. For there is a root of sinful self-interest in us that is at odds with a free spirit, just as the free spirit is incompatible with selfishness. These two ways of life are antithetical, so that you cannot live at times one way and at times another way according to how you feel on any given day.
> (Galatians 5:16-18, *The Message*)

The word 'sinful' sounds like it's serious, but it's really talking about the fleshly propensity we have for doing what we want.

When we think of this in relation to those frustrations while we wait, it shows the internal battle we have. But we have been given help; we have the Holy Spirit. This passage reminds us we need to be God-focused, not flesh-focused, in our frustrations. Otherwise, we can act out, we can react in our need and this may not always be wise for us. Following our flesh doesn't bring 'peace *and* well-being' into our daily lives (Philippians 4:9).

Irritations

The days continued to pass on the ark. So far, Noah and his family had lived together for nearly four months. Surely there would have been those little irritations that built up over time? What if Emzara liked to put more salt in the dishes Tia cooked? What if Mert watched Sarah sew a tapestry and always told her how she could make it better? Besides their own emotional states, doubts and concerns, the women had to cope with the consequences of their behaviour on each other.

Again, feeling irritated while we wait is natural. Here in the UK, it's a very British thing to queue while we are waiting to be served in a shop. If there is a long line, people tend to get irritated; we hear them mutter about all the different reasons why the queue isn't moving fast enough. Some people push in to get ahead; they just can't wait.

Waiting is hard.

I get irritated when the Wi-Fi connection plays up and a videocall with my friends disconnects. In my irritation I find myself rushing to get it working quickly again and therefore often end up taking more time than if I were to just calmly work through the steps.

So, longer waiting is even harder for our irritation levels. The longer we wait the more stressed we get, and the easier it is for those frustrations and irritations to manifest themselves. We get short-tempered and snappy. Irritation is in the same camp as frustration. Why? Because both of them link to anger.

We get angry with ourselves. We get angry at others. We get angry at God.

It's not easy in the flesh to control irritation: 'Short-tempered people do foolish things' (Proverbs 14:17, NLT). I find I'm unable to stop myself when I'm irritated. I can spot it afterwards, or even when I'm in mid-flow, but when we are irritated we always want someone else to know. What often bubbles over is a false kind of irritation with them, when we're actually irritated with ourselves or something else. Irritation, like anger, can be damaging when we wait.

So what do we do, then? Can we be 'People with understanding [who] control their anger' (Proverbs 14:29, NLT, addition mine)? What is this understanding we have?

Well, we have the understanding of the Holy Spirit being with us. If you're a believer then you'll be familiar with the fruits of the Holy Spirit.[26] I have incorrectly thought that because I have the Holy Spirit in me, who gives us these fruits, that I *should* have all these traits without having to do anything. So when I don't behave in that way, I feel bad. That's when Satan sees a perfect opportunity to come and lie to me, to try to deceive me about my relationship with God, that somehow I'm letting Him down. I feel that shame. The weight of sin starts to burden me again. I think, 'Will I ever get it? Will I ever behave in the way I *should*?'

I think this is when God, as our Father, would like to tap us on the shoulder and say, 'Let Me just give you a hug. It's OK, I know you're not going to always get it here on earth. I know you feel snappy and hot-tempered, I know you've messed up again, but My love for you remains. And when you're here in heaven, yes, you'll be transformed, there won't be these fleshly struggles. But in the meantime, let Me just love you for who you are right now.'

Going down that line of thinking really irritates Satan, and that's an acceptable form of irritation, by the way! The enemy doesn't want us thinking that way. Why? Because Satan doesn't

---

[26] The fruits of the Spirit are 'love, joy, peace, patience, kindness, goodness, faithfulness, gentleness, and self-control' (Galatians 5:22-23, NLT).

want us having the reassurance of our Father's love, His peace and wholeness. He wants to do anything to make us feel burdened and oppress us even more while we wait; to get us caught up in the feelings.

The truth is, we do have the fruits of the Holy Spirit in our lives. We do have all of these traits in us because of Him. That's the promise. That's the supernatural transformation which happened when we gave our lives to Jesus. 'We are living by the Spirit' (Galatians 5:25, NLT).

So when I'm feeling irritated, that's when I really need self-control, one of the fruits, but it isn't just there. Galatians 5:22 says, 'the Holy Spirit produces this kind of fruit in our lives' (NLT). 'Produces' – that's present tense. The Holy Spirit hasn't *produced* self-control in my life. 'Produces' is about a constant state of growth.

I'm learning that I need to tend the right tree. I need to live by the Holy Spirit to allow Him to develop and ripen that fruit within me. As we learn to live more and more with Him, we'll find this fruit will flourish. As we look away from what our flesh wants, and choose to nurture the relationship with Him, so we will find the fruits of the Spirit manifesting in our lives.

We're not going to avoid expectations, frustrations and irritations while we wait. Some of these may not be bad things either, like the expectations we have in the Lord. As we go through those waiting circumstances, we can work with the Holy Spirit in us to help produce the fruit we need during that particular time. And one of those we especially need while we're still waiting is patience. I wonder how the women's patience levels were on the ark? As month four came to an end, did they wonder if they would ever leave?

Timing

Outside the ark, floodwaters prevailed. The earth was covered and the water had risen over the mountain peaks by 'fifteen cubits' (Genesis 7:20) which is about 23ft or 7m. Next time you see a mountain, picture water 23ft or 7m high above it, and the ark floating over the top. That would be quite a sight.

Even if Noah were to have thought, 'It's time, we've waited long enough,' he couldn't leave. Noah had no control or influence over their wait.

Why did God make everything wait on the ark? Once the flood had completed its purpose, God could have made the waters quickly retreat, the ark settle, couldn't He? I think it comes down to the mystery of His timings. We find ourselves frequently asking during our waiting times, 'Why, Lord?'

The longer we wait, the harder it gets. In comes rush, pace and pressure. I want to take over the driving seat, to have control. I don't have time to hang around for answers. I can't wait any more. How easy is it for us to have these thoughts even though we know we need to wait on the Lord?

Sometimes waiting doesn't make sense. It also depends on what we're waiting for, whether it's a *sense of soon* the Lord has placed in our hearts, something we want that's material, or a change in our life or someone else's. Sometimes we may not even see the evidence of what we're waiting for; sometimes we need a great deal of patience.

This makes me think of Abraham. In Genesis 12 we read about the early years of God's call on Abraham's life. He had just left his family and was travelling with his wife and nephew. They went through the land of Canaan, 'Then the LORD appeared to Abram[27] and said, "I will give this land to your descendants"'(Genesis 12:7).

God was making a promise here, but Abraham would have needed to stay a very long time by the massive tree to see it materialise (Genesis 12:6). He could have said to the Lord, 'I'm just going to sit here and wait for this to happen,' but he didn't. Instead, he continued to move forward and progress; it wasn't a wait for him to enter into. Yet, as we read about him, we see how God led him and worked in his life. Abraham didn't live to

---

[27] This was his name until the Lord changed it to Abraham (Genesis 17:5).

see his descendants in the land, but God still brought about the promise.

This was another waiting time for God too. Another time for God to be patient and to wait until He could give the land to Abraham's offspring. This reminds me how, in those before-the-flood days, God patiently waited. So far, during the months on the ark, they'd all had to be patiently waiting too.

Is it good for us in any waiting to get impatient and try to hasten things forward? Paul says, 'But if we hope for what we do not see, we wait eagerly for it with patience *and* composure' (Romans 8:25). Somehow I don't think the patience and composure Paul speaks about here means we should be falling over ourselves in a desire to push forward the wait. We need to patiently wait and be self-controlled and calm while we're waiting. Perhaps something that will help while we patiently wait is that we can, as Paul says 'wait eagerly'?

Because Paul's not saying here that we have to go about soberly while we're waiting, like it's a struggle; we can wait with anticipation. And that's because our faith hasn't gone; like Abraham had to trust in the promise God made, yet still continue to travel; like Noah and his family had to wait on the ark for a sign from God. We have to trust in God's timings. We trust with expectation and eagerness while relying on another fruit the Holy Spirit produces – patience. So, with Him, we can learn to be patient in the waiting, patient with our wants and we can learn to be satisfied (Philippians 4:11).

Feeling forgotten in the wait

It was the start of the fifth month now on the ark and nothing had changed.

Think about Tia and Sarah walking around the corridors, talking about what they could cook with lentils again. The lack of anything happening over the past months worried them and they shared their concerns. Abruptly the ark swayed from side to side, sharply lurching so they bumped into each other. When they got up from the floor, shaken and bruised, something had altered. The ark wasn't moving. The swaying had stopped:

> And God remembered *and* thought kindly of Noah and every living thing and all the animals that were with him in the ark; and God made a wind blow over the land, and the waters receded. Also the fountains of the deep [subterranean waters] and the windows of the heavens were closed, the [pouring] rain from the sky was restrained, and the waters receded steadily from the earth. At the end of a hundred and fifty days the waters had diminished. On the seventeenth day of the seventh month [five months after the rain began], the ark came to rest on the mountains of Ararat [in Turkey].
> (Genesis 8:1-4)

We can feel that God has forgotten us when we're waiting, that He hasn't heard our prayers, or we doubt His promises. Thinking about how we are as women, I don't think it's unlikely that at some point Noah's family felt that God had forgotten them. But in these verses we see that 'God remembered'. Of course, God hadn't literally forgotten them, but what He was doing here was setting in place the motions needed so they could leave. These actions happened before the ark came to rest among the mountains. God didn't just pull out a plug and all the floodwaters immediately drained; they 'receded steadily'.

The women couldn't see the world outside. For five months their vision had been restricted to wooden walls. They didn't know the dangers of the water surrounding them. Yes, the rain stopped after forty days and nights, but God needed to close 'the fountains of the deep' and 'the windows of the heavens'. He also needed to stop the rain from pouring again. Remember, as soon as the first droplet fell, rain was introduced to the earth. Weather systems that hadn't been around at the time of Adam and Eve had now been established. Grey skies would be as common as blue in the post-flood earth.

Though there may have been no evidence of His hand during all those months, and a lack of apparent signs, God was working while they waited, and the waters decreased enough for the ark's base to find one of the solid mountain peaks it had been floating over. How often do we feel ignored in our wait? Forgotten by God?

More times than not there can be little evidence of His hand working in our circumstances which we so want and need to be changed. Yet, like outside the ark, He's working. We may just not understand all the reasons why; all the pieces have yet to be put into place. How many times does the wait keep us from unseen dangers? When we look back with hindsight we can realise if we'd tried to push the wait, to make something happen, it wouldn't have helped us in the way we thought it would.

The ark was a place of safety. A resting space among the chaos of the natural events outside. We need to be able to *allow ourselves to rest* while God works. 'Let all that I am wait quietly before God, for my hope is in him' (Psalm 62:5, NLT).

We need to constantly encourage ourselves while we're waiting that there is action being taken on our behalf and we need to trust in the Lord. He has not forgotten us.

Waiting with the Lord

In the last chapter we learned about Jesus understanding our emotions of worry and anxiety. He's not afraid to call them out. Do we forget during the times of our want and wait that Jesus understands those emotions we encounter? That we can be safe and release them to Him, or instead do we try to be perfect during the wait? So if we're not pushing to try to control the wait, we're trying to work out how we *should* be waiting?

We're weary, and so much more so when we're waiting in our own efforts. The compassion of the Lord steps in, though, and tells us, 'You might be tired, but I'll give you My strength':

He energizes those who get tired,
gives fresh strength to dropouts.

For even young people tire and drop out,
young folk in their prime stumble and fall.
But those who wait upon GOD get fresh strength.
They spread their wings and soar like eagles,
They run and don't get tired,
they walk and don't lag behind.
(Isaiah 40:29-31, *The Message*)

When we wait with God, He gives us 'fresh strength'. He doesn't make us hold out using up every last drop of our own efforts. Instead, when we are waiting on Him to work, He keeps us supplied. And besides the strength to wait, the verses speak to me about the movement we experience while we wait. What do I mean?

Well, waiting doesn't mean we're stuck in the same spot. While everyone waited on the ark it was still travelling over the floodwaters. The family still had to get up and eat, feed the animals. We still have to go about our everyday lives. We have to live through each day. And if one day feels like it's a running pace, we won't get tired. If another feels like a long uphill walk, we won't lag. It is only the Lord's strength that can increase our power of patience in the wait; only the Lord who can help us to be victorious while we're waiting for outcomes, while we're waiting for the answers to our large, medium and small-scale wants.

Can we be happy in the wait?

After the sign of the ark resting, Emzara might have felt a familiar returning worry about another unknown, just like when the rain stopped but they hadn't immediately left the ark. However, with this sign came new information that the floodwaters outside were changing. No longer were they in this semi-suspended state where they didn't know what was going on. But where were they? When could they leave?

The days continued to roll on, into the sixth month, then the seventh month of being on the ark. Were the women happy during their wait? We don't know, but can we be happy when we're waiting?

We know happiness is a feeling, and what makes us happy doesn't necessarily come from what we need or desire. Happiness can be as fleeting as a ray of sunshine before a cloud passes over. You can be happily eating a piece of cake, but during the next mouthful your phone rings with bad news. When we have those happy times, then we can embrace and fully experience the moments, but we don't want to rely on them as a measure for our lives. I think it's unlikely we'll always be happy while we wait, and neither should we feel bad if we aren't. But can we be joyful when we are feeling confused?

Well, joy is totally different from happiness, especially when we think of it in relation to the Lord. As we search through our Bibles, we find so many verses about joy. This can be in the context of when we praise the Lord and give a joyful exclamation (Psalm 71:23), but God also speaks about joy in relation to us – 'the joy of the LORD [being our] strength' (Nehemiah 8:10, addition mine).

In our human state, do we need strength when we're feeling joyful? No. We need strength when we feel the opposite, when we're waiting. So what is this joy Nehemiah 8:10 refers to?

It's not something that can be manufactured; it comes from the Lord. We don't need to make a special request to obtain it, because we were given His joy when we gave our lives to Jesus. The joy we have from Jesus is our salvation; the confidence and certainty that come from our lives being in Him. It is the Holy Spirit in us who manifests this joy, yet another one of those fruits He produces.

When we thought about faith, we talked about how we can't always physically sense it, and joy can be like that. Having this kind of joy doesn't mean we're walking around with a false smile on our faces when we're hurting. We can live each day joyfully in Him even when we don't feel it. We can joyfully praise the Lord at all times, letting the joy of knowing our Saviour fill and overwhelm us, as we fix our eyes back on Him. Then in comes

His strength and His reassurance, and His joy supersedes happiness every time.

Nearly eight months and still waiting

Inside the ark, routines would have had to continue, while outside the waters would have continued to decrease. Everything aboard the ark had had no other choice than to wait until 'on the first day of the tenth month' mountain peaks were visible (Genesis 8:5). The Bible doesn't tell us who saw the mountains around the ark or how they were seen. So why is this verse there?

I think it's another reminder to encourage us about the ongoing unseen action by God while Noah and his family waited. That perhaps, though they may not have had any of their wants materialise in the wait, God had been working.

We'll also experience this, whether we've been waiting for eight days, eight months or eight years. We can try to figure out why things haven't happened. We may realise that, actually, what we thought we wanted we don't need any more. With the passing of time we may realise why we've had to wait.

When there's no choice other than to wait, it doesn't mean we're not moving forward. We can choose to be led by the Spirit to not allow those fleshly frustrations and irritations to control us. Though there may be no evidence, God's still working in our lives, and it's all about His timing. We can wait expectantly. We can wait joyfully. We can wait eagerly. We trust in the Lord:

> This I recall to my mind,
> Therefore I have hope.
> *Through* the LORD'S mercies we are not consumed,
> Because His compassions fail not.
> *They are* new every morning;
> Great *is* Your faithfulness.
> 'The LORD *is* my portion,' says my soul,
> 'Therefore I hope in Him!'
> The LORD *is* good to those who wait for Him,

To the soul *who* seeks Him.
(Lamentations 3:21-25, NKJV)

*Father, so often I find myself coming to You with a need, with
something I lack. Help me to remember that You are 'my
Shepherd [and] I shall not want'.*[28] *I know I've waited many
times before for You to answer and I know I'll need to wait
again. Thank You that You are working, even if I can't see,
hear or feel it. Throughout Your Word, You give me
encouragement to wait expectantly, to wait confidently, to
remember Your love is 'new every morning'.*[29] *Even while I
wait You will give me strength and I'm joyful in my salvation.
Jesus, I lay down how I feel at the moment and leave it for
You to work on everything. You know all my thoughts and
frustrations and what I truly need.*
Amen.

---

[28] Psalm 23:1, NKJV.
[29] Lamentations 3:23.

Chapter contemplations

- Find out more about waiting in the Bible. Use a concordance to find some verses or read about others who waited, like Joseph. Share your thoughts with a friend.

- Remind yourself when nothing is happening while you wait that God is working. Be hopeful in Him. Be proactive with the Holy Spirit when you feel those frustrations and irritations. Be led by Him so He can produce those fruits found in Galatians 5 in your life.

- Reflect on all the times you've waited before, and what those waiting times might have kept you from. Spend some time writing down your reflections in your journal.

Journal pages

7

A Raven and a Dove

With the mountaintops now visible, was Noah closer to being able to open the ark's window? And if so, what was its purpose?

The ark's window

When God told Noah to build the ark, God gave him specifications, which included some information about the window. The window was to be set 18in or 46cm from the top of the ark. However, it doesn't say in the Bible how wide or deep the window was, but I think it had to be of a relative size to the ark's proportions to bring the necessary 'light and ventilation' which God speaks about in Genesis 6:16.

We don't know how many times Noah opened and shut the window during their months on the ark, or whether it was even unfastened at all up until this time. But we do know from Genesis 8:5-6 that once the mountain peaks were obvious, the window wasn't opened for forty days. If it was me, I'd have kept wanting to look out of the window and check what was happening. So why did Noah have to wait?

Forty days

Noah and his family had been waiting for all those months, and now, just when a glimpse of change was given to them, they had to continue to wait. We know there are many other instances in the Bible where the number 40 is mentioned, such as Jesus being tested in the desert 'for forty days and forty nights' (Matthew 4:2) and the 'forty years' the Israelites wandered around the desert (Joshua 5:6). But here in this story, these forty days of waiting sound similar to the forty days of rain that fell at the beginning of their journey. They had to wait for forty days while the rain poured onto the earth. Now as their time on the ark drew to completion, there was another wait, another effort to hold on. This time, though, the forty days were about the floodwaters outside decreasing rather than increasing.

I don't think it's a coincidence that Genesis 8:6 tells us, 'Noah opened the window of the ark *which he had made*' (italics mine). It reminds us, the readers, that this time it was Noah who took the action to unfasten the ark's window. Whereas God had safely shut the ark's door behind them nearly nine months earlier when they had first entered the ark, now it was safe for Noah to open the ark's window into the outside world.

The sense of anticipation during those forty days must have been intense. Everyone must have felt something was going to happen; they just didn't know exactly what. As the pressure of the water on the earth lowered, did the pressure inside the ark build? Would Noah opening the ark's window release it?

Our windows

When we think of windows, they allow light to enter a room. They frame the surroundings beyond them. You might, like me, when you go out in the evening, find yourself drawn to briefly look through people's downstairs windows when they haven't shut the curtains. Even if you're driving past in a car, you get a snapshot of a moment – people watching television, a person moving around their kitchen. We're drawn to windows; we want to look out of them and into them. When I stay in a hotel room or explore a historic house, the first thing I do is go towards the window, to look at the view.

Windows allow us to see out. They allow others to see in. Besides the physical boundaries windows give to our buildings, we have personal windows. What do I mean? Well, windows in our lives can be:

- How much we choose to open up and let in, or how we much we shut out. Sometimes we allow our windows to open up to others a tiny little bit. Sometimes we push them back to their full extent. Sometimes we don't want to open them at all.

- A limited frame of what's going on around us, just like we can look out of a window and know it's autumn because we see the leaves falling. The windows of our lives give us a picture of change coming. If I were to lean out of my window right now (and I wouldn't recommend doing that!), I can only see a certain distance. However, I can still see something, and sometimes we discern a development, whether that's from what we witness in reality or what we sense.

Taking action in either of these examples causes us to feel something.

We may want to fling open our window to share something with someone, but this particular window in our lives hasn't been opened for a while and it's sticky. It's one of those windows we have to force. We know we want to push the window open, but can we?

We may sense a change coming and find ourselves clinging to the window latch. Though we might have eagerly been looking for a development, when we catch sight of it we're scared. It's the act of letting in an unknown element to our current state.

Opening our windows to change

When we pull back the curtains and open up a window in our lives, we're allowing our present state to be altered. We're both releasing pressure and letting in the light, air and sounds beyond the glass protecting us from the elements. In reality, we wouldn't open the windows in our home when there's a snowstorm outside.

Yes, it may be an unconscious decision to do this in our own home, but in our lives, opening our window exposes our vulnerability. We have to let go and take the risk of what might fly in – a bee or a butterfly?

So, how do we react when we discern that change? When we catch sight of a new season coming into our lives?

'It depends what the change is,' I hear you say. Indeed. Often we don't have a choice as to whether we open the window up to it or not. Remember, though, we're just catching sight of change from our window; this isn't the full picture, or walking completely into it.

When we have to open our window

When we have to open our window on to something we may not like, or we know isn't going to be easy, that can be a difficult thing to do. It reminds me of a time when a family member was taken ill unexpectedly. We had the phone call, the sense that something serious was happening, but didn't quite know what. And we had to throw open our window on to the change of seeing them clearly unwell, then an ambulance being called, the hospital tests, the talks from doctors, arranging end-of-life care. All those steps began with that momentary, sudden flash of lightning seen from behind the window pane.

This makes me think of Daniel in the Bible. The high officers in King Darius' kingdom were jealous of Daniel's success and tried to find a way to accuse and bring him down. They convinced the king to establish a law that if anyone was caught praying in the next thirty days to any god or man except the king himself, they would be thrown into the lions' den. Those high officers weren't stupid; they knew Daniel had faith and that he prayed to his God. So they thought this was the perfect way to end his life (Daniel 6:1-9). What did Daniel do?

When he heard about the new law, that's when he caught sight of the change coming. Up until then, he wouldn't have had to think about whether he was safe or not when he prayed. Now, with this law, he had a choice. If Daniel chose to open up his window, literally and metaphorically, then he wasn't going to enter an easy time. However, Daniel didn't think twice:

> Now when Daniel knew that the document was signed, he went into his house (now in his roof chamber his *windows were open* toward Jerusalem); he continued to get down on his knees three times a day, praying and giving thanks before his God, as he had been doing previously. (Daniel 6:10, italics mine)

Daniel not only chose to make himself visible by sitting in front of the window, but he also made his prayers heard. Of course, the high officers knew where he lived and they made sure they passed his home. When they reported his law-breaking to King Darius, he wasn't happy about enacting the law, but he had no choice, and Daniel was thrown into the lions' den (Daniel 6:11-17).

There are two things which I think are important to consider before we get to what happened with Daniel in the den. Firstly, when the high officers went to his home, they saw Daniel calling to the Lord (Daniel 6:11). See, when Daniel knew he had to open the window, he not only prayed, but also asked for God's help for what was going to happen next. Remember, he'd had a glimpse, with this knowledge about the new law, but he hadn't caught sight of the full extent; he didn't know exactly what would occur. Either way, Daniel wasn't going to rely on his own strength; he knew he needed God's help.

Secondly, the king wasn't ignorant; he knew what his high officers had done when they came back and reported Daniel, but because of the law he'd signed he couldn't stop what had to happen. However, the king knew Daniel was a man of faith, and before Daniel was thrown into the den, he said, 'May your God, whom you constantly serve, rescue you Himself!' (Daniel 6:16).

He knew Daniel needed a rescuer, someone who could step in and save Daniel from inevitable death at the lions' jaws. Daniel didn't get saved immediately; he still had to go through the trial of being with the lions. He still had to experience the consequences of opening the window, but God was with Daniel. God was with him when he prayed and asked for strength. God was with him when he spent the night with the lions.

God is with us when we spot those thunder clouds rolling in. God is with us when we have to open our window on to something we don't like.

He has promised, 'I will never fail you. I will never abandon you' (Hebrews 13:5, NLT). Though we may have opened the window, God's never going to open up His hand and let go of us.

So what happened to Daniel?

He left the lions' den in the morning and 'no injury whatever was found on him, because he believed in *and* relied on *and* trusted in his God' (Daniel 6:23). The high officers and their families ended up in the lions' den themselves. King Darius sent a message throughout his vast empire praising the Lord and declaring God as the one who 'rescues and saves' (Daniel 6:27).

Daniel could never have predicted when he opened the window all that he would go through and that God would use it to His glory. It couldn't have been easy being cast into the den, and spending the night with lions, even though God sent an angel to restrain them (Daniel 6:22). Going through the stressful circumstances not only gave Daniel the assurance of trusting in the Lord, but it was also a testimony to His faithfulness. A testimony that was used to encourage and witness to many others.

Though the challenge of opening our window may not always be easy or what we want to do, we can be strengthened by trusting God. That way, even as we go to push it open, we can pray to Him for help, like Daniel did, and know that whatever happens, God isn't going to let us go.

When we want to open our window, but...

Sometimes there can be a natural fear when we think of windows. We wouldn't let a child go near an open window on the first floor. We lock our windows to secure against people breaking into our homes. We put up curtains or coverings to give us privacy. We have control about what we choose to do with them.

So when we think of opening a window in our life to a change we want, how do we feel? Let's remind ourselves again that we're glimpsing a limited view, not the full picture. Though we may want to move forward into that next step so much, we find ourselves caught behind the window, our hand on its catch, frozen, unable to move. Why?

Because we can be afraid to open ourselves up to change. We're entering into a state of losing control, of not knowing what will happen, and fear paralyses us. I wonder what Noah thought when he passed by the ark's window during the forty days of waiting to open it?

He couldn't escape the window, it was there on the third deck, but this time he knew from the Lord he would have to open it. Surely Noah must have felt some trepidation about what he'd see outside? About what that vista would lead to? They'd been on the ark for nearly nine months and I think they would have grown comfortable in their situation. Yes, they may not have wanted to live on the ark for the rest of the lives, but the reality of thinking about leaving the ark, and all those unknowns ahead, would, I believe, have been daunting.

A couple of years ago there was some talk about changes happening in the department I worked in; these involved potential voluntary redundancies. I had been praying about what to do next; there had been a lot going on in my personal life, and I felt that familiar sense of needing to make a move. With this news, I caught sight of something, and as the talk progressed into entering into an official process, I felt that I wanted to open the window, but I was scared.

Yes, I was naturally unsure, because putting myself forward for voluntary redundancy could create a significant change. At this stage when I opened the window to consider the possibility, I didn't even know whether it would happen. All I knew was that besides my own thoughts that it was something I wanted to do, there was a whisper, that 'still small voice' (1 Kings 19:12, NKJV) from God saying it was time.

As I followed the process over the months, it eventually reached the point where I was offered the choice. What I caught sight of through the window this time was more than an opportunity. I lifted the blind and saw the bright green buds on the branches; the signs of a new season coming. Now, in reality, we don't have a choice to stop the seasons, whether we like or don't like the change we observe. But for me, with this offer, I still could have shut the window on those signs of change; I did have a choice.

I'd been blessed in my career, had a great team and achieved a lot. In one way, it didn't make sense to leave all of the future possibilities and the financial security of the role. I could sense the Lord asking me to step into something different, even though I didn't know what that was, and I felt trepidatious.

But that fear we have when we feel change, when we know we need to allow ourselves to take the next step – that may not always be natural. Satan would like nothing better than to stop us from opening the window to hold us back in the *what-was-once* instead of *what-with-God-might-be*:

> our struggle is not against flesh and blood [contending only with physical opponents], but against the rulers, against the powers, against the world forces of this [present] darkness, against the spiritual *forces* of wickedness in the heavenly (supernatural) *places*.
> (Ephesians 6:12)

The '[present] darkness' pulls down the blind and shuts out the breeze, and we grow heavy under the weight of the oppression.

I could have easily frozen when I made my decision, but I felt a peace and accepted the offer. However, it didn't stop the enemy from attacking me while I worked out my notice time. Satan did everything he could to make me doubt myself, throwing those accusatory questions[30] to make me feel fearful of the future, and that it would be better to just stay: it would be safer.

You know the enemy isn't going to be nice and quietly whisper during those times when we spot a change coming. Satan's always on the prowl like a lion ready to pounce (1 Peter 5:8), but just like God gave Daniel safety in the lions' den, He gives us help too.

Against the 'darkness' and paralysis from all the fear comes:

Light, space, zest –
that's GOD!
So, with him on my side I'm fearless,
afraid of no one and nothing.
(Psalm 27:1, *The Message*)

The truth is, Jesus on the cross defeated the darkness when He cried, 'It is finished!' (John 19:30). At that point when Jesus died, there was no power for Satan to have a hold against us. Death lost its sting. Jesus has already won the victory, and He gives us victory in our lives (1 Corinthians 15:55,57). Until Satan is finally cast down into hell (Revelation 20:10), we live in this world, with its 'present darkness', with an enemy who knows he's on limited time, and wants to rob as much of our lives as he can.

If I'd stayed focused on the fear I felt during those months, I would have crippled myself. I wouldn't have been open to the possibilities that awaited from taking such a big step. The Lord was good, and He brought reassurance and encouragement into those days, from meeting people who'd already taken such a decision and progressed into other careers, to being able to start to consider making the trip to America, that *sense of soon* potentially occurring. All of these and more shone a light against

---

[30] Satan is an accuser as stated in Revelation 12:10.

the darkness Satan wanted to wrap around me. Jesus is the 'Light of the world' (John 8:12), and it is His light we need to shine into our fear-filled rooms, so that He can warm us with His victory, His promises. There is no space in light for darkness to hide.

When you catch sight of that change and it's leading you into something different, something you feel at peace with Him to want to move into, then don't allow yourself to be paralysed. Don't find yourself caught, unable to even lift back the blind. Don't be afraid of the words Satan whispers. Remember, as you go to push open the window, Jesus is on your side. He's right there with you, and He'll stay with you, as the pressure changes from opening yourself up to what's out there, as Jesus leads you into the bigger picture only He knows about.

When Noah opened the ark's window

The end of the fortieth day approached; soon Noah would be opening the ark's window not only to take a look but also to release one of the birds they'd cared for over the past months. Besides giving a glimpse of what lay beyond and around the ark, opening the widow had another purpose:

> At the end of [another] forty days Noah opened the
> window of the ark which he had made; and he sent out
> a raven, which flew here and there until the waters were
> dried up from the earth.
> (Genesis 8:6-7)

We're not told when Noah made the decision about sending out a raven, whether this was something Noah debated while he waited, or a decision he took on the fortieth day. Again I think Noah must have sensed from the Lord that he needed to take the action to look outside and also gain understanding about what was happening with the floodwaters.

A raven

There must have been so many different kinds of birds to pick from in the ark, and other animals or insects that flew too. So why did Noah choose a raven? Perhaps he was aware of the raven's ability to sense direction?

If we were considering what kind of bird would give us insight about whether it was safe to go outside, a raven would be a good choice. Ravens are extremely clever, and historically mariners have used them at sea.[31] Raven are also large birds and skilled at flying.[32]

Let's just step back here and remind ourselves that for months nothing had left the ark. This was going to be the first time something exited. So as well as the practical considerations, we also need to think about what this choice of bird might mean symbolically.

There are a variety of interpretations across different cultures about ravens, but there is often a sense of something mystical about them; about ravens being messengers of something not good. In literature, ravens are often used to represent death.[33] At the Tower of London there is a legend that if the ravens were to go, then the realm would come down.[34] In the Bible, ravens are unclean birds and forbidden as food (Deuteronomy 14:11-14).

---

[31] Amelia Stymacks, 'Why Ravens and Crows are Earth's Smartest Birds', *National Geographic*, 15th March 2018,
www.nationalgeographic.com/news/2018/03/year-of-the-bird-brains-intelligence-smarts/ (accessed 20th October 2020). Ruddy Cano, 'How sailors navigated before GPS', Mighty History, We Are The Mighty, 29th April 2020, www.wearethemighty.com/mighty-history/navigating-sea-before-gps-vikings/ (accessed 20th October 2020).
[32] 'Common Raven', *National Geographic*,
www.nationalgeographic.com/animals/birds/c/common-raven/ (accessed 20th October 2020).
[33] Edgar Allan Poe, 'The Raven', 'Death and the Afterlife Theme Analysis', *Litcharts*, www.litcharts.com/lit/the-raven/themes/death-and-the-afterlife (accessed 20th October 2020).
[34] 'The ravens', Tower of London, www.hrp.org.uk/tower-of-london/whats-on/the-ravens/#gs.imfux5 (accessed 20th October 2020).

Imagine Noah as he made his way up the ladder to the window on the third deck with a raven on his arm. Noah leaned against the frame he'd made a long time ago and took deep breaths, relishing the sensation of the wind. The breeze against his face. The raven squawked, eager to stretch its wings. For a moment the raven sat there on Noah's arm before it took off. Black wings rose up and down over the floodwaters surrounding the ark. The first bird to be released disappeared from Noah's view.

Noah must have had a lot to cogitate on. He'd already had to wait until the end of the fortieth day, and now he knew there were still floodwaters around, but what would the raven find? The bird didn't come back to the ark, though; instead, it 'flew here and there until the waters were dried up from the earth' (Genesis 8:7). We know the raven had the ability to find its way back to the security of the ark. Yet that raven chose to use its intelligence to fly around the mountaintops.

God created the raven, so this doesn't take away from it being a beautiful bird and part of His creation. Whatever motivated Noah to make his choice, I don't think it's accidental, that with everything the raven symbolically represents, that this bird was chosen to fly out of the ark's window. Something that was unclean needed to leave first. I wonder whether Noah anticipated that the raven wouldn't return. Why? Because he didn't wait for the raven to fly back. Noah didn't think, 'I'll go to bed and see what happens in the morning.' No, he went to the bird compartments, but this time Noah didn't return for the other raven; instead, he went to another bird perch and made his way back to the window (Genesis 8:8).

Why did Noah then choose a dove?

This time Noah chose a bird from a different family:

> Then Noah sent out a dove to see if the water level had fallen below the surface of the land. But the dove found no place on which to rest the sole of her foot, and she

returned to him to the ark, for the waters were [still] on the face of the entire earth. So he reached out his hand and took the dove, and brought her into the ark. (Genesis 8:8-9)

The dove was a complete contrast to the raven, and this time we're also told the bird's gender.

What's also significant is that since Noah released this bird from the ark's window, doves have remained a strong symbol throughout history.[35] We think of them as a sign of peace, with their brilliant, pure feathers; they are an image often used on Christmas cards. A dove embodies the feeling of hope, and the hope brought from God. In the Bible, when Jesus was baptised the 'Holy Spirit descended ... in bodily form like a dove' (Luke 3:22). They are also ritually clean birds, unlike the raven.

So, after the raven, light flew from the ark in the shape of a dove, but she found nowhere peaceful to land. The floodwaters with all their dangers rippled around the ark. This time Noah did not have to think about whether the bird would return; she flew back to Noah's outstretched arm.

We're not told whether anyone was with Noah when he opened the window and released the birds. Did he do this task alone to protect the family? Maybe he realised the weight of expectation it would place on them and he wanted to see what happened first. But after the adventure of opening and shutting the window, releasing not just one bird, but two, we can imagine Noah not being able to hold the news in and wanting to share it with Emzara. If she were to expectantly ask him, 'When will you send the dove again?' she would need to prepare herself because Noah would say he wouldn't be releasing the dove again for another seven days.

Another, another, another... wait.

[35] Dorothy Willette, 'The Enduring Symbolism of Doves', *Bible History Daily*, 1st January 2021, www.biblicalarchaeology.org/daily/ancient-cultures/daily-life-and-practice/the-enduring-symbolism-of-doves/ (accessed 8th January 2021).

Seven days

Like the forty days Noah had to wait before he opened the window, I don't think this waiting period was a random number. We know the number seven is a holy number. It was on the seventh day that God 'rested' after He created the world (Genesis 2:2). God gave Noah the seven-day warning He was going to send the flood (Genesis 7:4). Again, I think the week of waiting had a purpose. Did it allow the family time to adjust to what was coming?

After all their months filled with the familiarity of a routine, there was no denying now that their days inside were numbered, as the ark's window was opened and shut. They'd had those glimpses outside, the confirmation that the waters were continuing to recede, but they couldn't yet leave.

We've talked about how we get these glimpses through windows in our lives. We see a possibility, our senses fill with new sensations. The window shuts. We know the answer is out there. We yearn to rush, but we can't; it's not quite the time.

We know the ark's window had a purpose. But I don't think God told Noah to build the window simply out of a design point of view. I think the window is part of the Genesis story to show us how many times Noah had to open and shut it on to the world outside before God spoke again.

For the next seven days, all everyone could do on the ark was wait, and the window stayed shut.

Shutting our window

We've spoken about when we might feel afraid to open a window on to change, but what about when we shut our feelings up?

Sometimes it's easier to keep how we feel inside rather than to acknowledge our emotions to ourselves or others. Sound familiar? Hands up time again, I'm waving mine.

It's human to shut things in. Yet it's another thing that we can easily criticise ourselves for. I'm one of those people who find it hard to talk about their emotions. I can't meet with a friend for coffee and launch straight into how I'm feeling. Sometimes I'm not even sure how I feel. Sometimes I just want to forget how I feel and talk about something else! I take time to process.

We choose how much we want to open up with others. How much we want to let them into our inner space and thoughts. That's all part of how we protect ourselves and our families… it's natural… but we do need a balance. I know the danger of self-internalising my emotions and not releasing the pressure. Our pace of life makes it easier to skip the apparently insignificant. We busy ourselves to hide the hurt. We can't deal with it. Of course we can't; hurting is hard.

When you're hurting, when you can't handle the pressure. It's too much. It is, isn't it? I know, you need to read that sentence twice.

Sometimes it's too much or feels plain unfair. We get the sparkly sticker for the first period of waiting, think that's it, and then something else happens, and another, and another. Life continues to roll on so we can barely recover and we don't feel like we're winners. The familiar temptation to give up seems suddenly so much easier. We find our emotions leaking out into the negative talk, almost as if we want our words to weld the window shut, but at the same time we want it to open so much. We cry:

> I'm hurt and in pain;
> Give me space for healing, and mountain air.
> (Psalm 69:29, *The Message*)

We want to break out of the boundaries of what's going on in our lives, circumstances and how we feel. Just anything to give us that freedom of space. The clean 'mountain air'. The silence of those surroundings.

Yet at the same time we can feel ourselves closing into a tight little ball, scared to let anything in and disrupt our preciously balanced state. The windows are triple locked and the shutters are boarded up against them.

Though we know Jesus is light, and how good He is, we can keep ourselves shut to Him. In the verse above from Psalm 69, David is pouring out his troubles, he wants God to save him, he wants God to 'Answer right now!' (Psalm 69:17, *The Message*). David is being very honest with God about his feelings. He's not trying to package everything up to look pretty or keep it from Him.

We may also find it harder to share with Jesus if we find it hard to share with others; or, if we can say everything to our friends, we find it hard to repeat those same words to Him. Again it comes back to allowing ourselves to be open, and not being scared about what opening up will do. Releasing the words breaks the power and paralysis our feelings create. It unfurls us from that tight little ball. Healing can then enter, like fresh air.

And with Jesus really is the safest space to do so. It's part of learning to walk with Him, of trusting Him and knowing He will be sensitive with us. We, like David, can be so open with the Lord because we know He is 'tender and kind, not easily angered, immense in love' (Psalm 86:15, *The Message*).

We frequently hear this scripture at Christmas carol services:

> For to us a Child shall be born, to us a Son shall be given;
> And the government shall be upon His shoulder,
> And His name shall be called *Wonderful Counselor*,
> Mighty God,
> Everlasting Father, Prince of Peace.
> (Isaiah 9:6, italics mine)

Do we pay enough attention to the first name Jesus is called?
'Wonderful Counselor'.

What a wonderful name for this child of God, born into a people-filled world. What a name we need, every day.

When I think of a counsellor, I think of someone experienced in listening, who's learned skills and can give some objective advice. But Jesus isn't just going to be a listener, a person whose guidance we can trust; He's going to be 'wonderful' at it. The best. I don't need to book an appointment; I can talk to Him any time, anywhere.

I so need a wonderful listener in my life. Someone to whom I can talk unhindered. And when I'm speaking with Him, He's also giving me peace because He reigns over it. He is my 'Prince of Peace', always and forevermore.

Listening to others

Being truly listened to and having someone's full attention is precious. It's a blessing to have people in our lives we trust and can be open with, and for them to feel that way about us. Frequently, though, we may start out with the best intentions, but our thoughts tend to jump everywhere and we can miss what people say to us. Or we hurry the conversation forward because we want to get on to the next thing. How life makes us feel, with all of its demands, doesn't help.

Think about it. We're trying to cook a meal, think about everything we've got to do tomorrow and remember to buy a card for a friend's birthday, then a loved one wanders into the kitchen and starts talking. They leave, and then we think afterwards, what were they really talking about?

When a friend or loved one opens up their emotional window to us, how do we react?

With how the pace of life is for everyone, it's tempting to be hasty and think we know the solution to the problem our loved one is telling us. We blurt it out without having absorbed and heard what they are actually saying. I think, with all of our time pressures, even subconsciously we have a drive to get through what needs to be done, so in a conversation when we hear something that sounds like it needs to be sorted, we can feel a desire to tick it off our to-do list.

I also think we have an instinct to want to try to fix something that hurts or is causing distress. And often we believe we have an immediate answer, the right advice to give to a person. However, in those moments when someone is sharing their burdens with us before we open our mouth, we need to take a minute and whisper to the wonderful counsellor we know, 'Jesus, what can I say here? Is it the advice You want me to give?'

Despite the solutions we think we may have, perhaps all the person needs is to see Jesus in us by us being the best listener we can be.

I'm definitely, with the Lord's help, working on my listening skills. With this also comes listening to Him. Just like how we can react to others, we can also feel that in our relationship with Jesus.

I'm sure He is used to me interrupting many times or jumping ahead of what He's trying to say to me! Spending time listening to the Lord doesn't always result in Him speaking to me, but it's about being in that attentive state of mind, of being able to calm ourselves and say, 'Lord, I'm here.' He wants us to 'Be still' (Psalm 46:10) with Him, to rest in our relationship, to enjoy being in each other's company. We don't need to be in a dedicated prayer mode to listen to Him. If we're paying attention, His 'still small voice' (1 Kings 19:12, NKJV) comes through at many moments of the day. It's having ourselves always open to Him: 'Listen for GOD's voice in everything you do, everywhere you go' (Proverbs 3:6, *The Message*).

An olive leaf

Since Noah had first opened the window, it had been open and shut, open and shut, open and shut, open... but we're running ahead of ourselves here. Let's return to the seven-day wait since Noah had released the raven and dove. He went back to the bird compartment and clutched the cooing dove to his chest. Notice he didn't choose a different bird; he was content to remain with the dove. After Noah released her from the window, I don't think he stay and waited for her there. Why? Because in the verse below, we see the dove didn't return until later in the day:

> He waited another seven days and again sent the dove out from the ark. The dove came back to him in the evening, and there, in her beak, was a fresh olive leaf. So Noah knew that the water level had subsided from the earth.
> (Genesis 8:10-11)

See how 'The dove came back to him in the evening' – this suggests to me that the bird was released earlier in the day, so yet again there was more waiting.

Noah had to look after the animals and follow his usual routines while he wondered whether the dove would find anything from her flight. Would she even return? Were the family aware that the window had been opened and a bird released?

The hours passed. Picture Sarah as she cleaned out the bird areas again, Tia busying herself with painting pottery jars, Mert sorting and repacking her clothes, all of them with expectant thoughts about what might happen.

Then, later in the evening, Noah's shout could be heard; everyone rushed to find him on the third deck. Noah stood with the dove in one hand and in the other he waved something. The dove had brought a gift back for them in her beak. An olive leaf. Freshly plucked from the tree.

A tree whose branches were no longer swallowed up in water. A tree that was alive. Life existed outside the ark. The death-filled waters were retreating and the no-longer-flooded earth was nearly ready for them. God did not speak here, but 'Noah knew that the water level had subsided from the earth'.

The olive leaf was a powerful sign. Out of everything the dove could have chosen, the olive leaf means so much. The leaf came from a tree they knew. They could identify it – this gave Noah and his family reassurance; the earth would still be familiar. It also signified provision – the leaf was from a tree that they could use for food. If an olive tree existed outside, then what else did? When they stepped from the ark it would not be into a barren desert.

They had been on the ark for nine months, but there wasn't much time left in their journey aboard it. The ark's window had been opened, the raven and the dove had been allowed to fly out of it, and after the waiting came the hope of soon returning to the earth. The dove would be released again in another familiar-sounding seven days, but this time she wouldn't return; instead, peace would be flying over the land waiting to greet them when they left the ark.

For us, we may not always want to open the window, but we know God will be with us, helping us, just like He helped Daniel in the lions' den. When we catch sight of that change but fear paralyses us, we need to remind ourselves that Jesus has already defeated the darkness.

Fix your eyes on Him (Hebrews 12:2). Allow yourself to open up to God, to experience Him:

> Open your mouth and taste, open your eyes and see –
> how good GOD is.
> Blessed are you who run to him.
> (Psalm 34:8, *The Message*)

Father, thank You that Your Son, Jesus, is the 'bright Morning Star'[36] in my life, that His light and His love cast out my fears and free me. Help me to understand the enemy's tactics when he brings darkness, and that with You, I don't need to be afraid. Give me wisdom, when I catch sight of something happening, to understand Your timings, just like Noah with all those times of waiting to open the window. Help me when I have to go through change. Jesus, I want to talk to You more and more; help me to open up and listen to You.
Amen.

---

[36] Revelation 22:16.

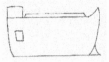

Chapter contemplations

- Spend some time journaling your thoughts about the windows in your life. How do you handle change?

- Read Psalm 69. Think about how honest David was in this psalm with God. Do you find it hard to open up your emotional window to Jesus? Speak to Him about it and trust Him to guide you as you start to share.

- Reflect about how you are when others open up to you. Pray for wisdom and resist the urge to immediately try to solve what they're saying, and listen.

Journal pages

8

God Remembers – the Rainbow

Aboard the ark, days passed since the last time the dove had been released and hadn't returned. We have increasing impetus but no exact timings. Noah was given an olive leaf by the bird, not a delivery plan of God's agenda contained within a scroll. Despite the palpable sense of the momentous change that was coming, each evening eight humans went to sleep, and each morning they awoke to another day.

What would come next?

Throughout their time on the ark, I'm sure the women supported each other, as they must have done before the flood. I wonder, in this period of waiting time, whether the women gave more attention to thinking about what their life would be like after the flood. There was no commission from God to collect and store food this time, no instructions about what was coming, yet there would have been practical necessities to consider.

As they went about the everyday moments, preparing another meal, checking the food supplies, stitching a tear in a gown, were there times when they all gathered at the table?

Their conversation could have started with Sarah telling them about the goats escaping out of their compartment, to Tia interrupting and asking Emzara whether they could plant roses before tomatoes. Then more questions. How would they manage the household? When should they set up the tents that were stored on the lower deck? Could they keep the flies, rabbits, birds and horses they all loved?

I don't believe the women wouldn't have thought about what would come next, even though they had no idea when or where that next would happen.

We know after Noah released the dove for the third time, 'she did not return' (Genesis 8:12). There doesn't seem to be any indication in the Bible that Noah expected to see the dove again. Instead, there was more than another month of waiting, despite the hope from the olive leaf.

As they entered a new year, then came action:

> Now in the six hundred and first year [of Noah's life], on the first day of the first month, the waters were drying up from the earth. Then Noah removed the covering of the ark and looked, and the surface of the ground was drying.
> (Genesis 8:13)

Rather than the ambiguousness of how the mountaintops had been seen three months before (Genesis 8:5), this is a clear step that Noah must have felt from the Lord to take. Following the action of removing the covering, Noah could clearly see that the flood was dissipating because the ground's surface was visible.

Isn't it amazing to see how all of these steps, right from when the ark rested against the mountains, have been gradually showing the family the changes in the level of the floodwaters?

When the dove plucked the leaf from the olive tree, it wouldn't have had water around its branches, but it still would have had water up to a level on its trunk. In Genesis 8:13 we're told that the actual ground, the earth's surface, was in a state of drying out, but it hadn't yet completely dried. Did they leave the ark on that day? No.

Again, notice how careful Noah was about this. He was patient, he didn't rush out of the ark, yet he must have wanted to – he could see ground that he hadn't seen for nearly a year! Instead, Noah had to trust in the timing of God. Here was Noah, at 601 years old, still being obedient.

Stepping into the unknown

We've spoken about encountering the unexpected, about how sometimes we're able to contextualise the circumstance against what we've done before, and sometimes we have nothing to centre our emotions on to, other than the Lord.

When Emzara and the women entered the ark, there were still unanswered questions. They bravely stepped into the safety of the ark, not knowing how long they would be aboard. The ark, though, was familiar to them, after having lived on it for such a long time. However, now with the earth drying and unknown land surrounding them, the prospect of leaving the ark must have felt daunting. A combination of excitement against nervousness. What would life be like in this new place? From the height of the third deck, Noah had perspective to take in the surroundings, but he was only able to look down at the ground. He wouldn't have been able to see all the detail as he would have done if he'd been standing on the land.

I think the time on the ark would have helped the women to work through their emotions about everything they'd left behind: the loss of their wider families, their homes. Though they would return to the earth where all that had been, none of it now existed. Another new beginning awaited them, and they would have to yet again step out into the unknown.

These are the grey areas, the uncertain places. The crossroads where we don't know whether we're turning right, left or going straight ahead. When we're moving towards something but we don't know quite what. We need courage to take those steps, but we need wisdom too. It's when we're in these uncertain places that we need wisdom the most, isn't it?

This is what strengthens and reassures us as we make our way towards a destination. And what's important to understand is that wisdom is shouting out to us during those times. Wisdom seeks to be heard to give us 'Common sense … success … Insight and strength' (Proverbs 8:14, NLT).

> Listen as Wisdom calls out!
> Hear as understanding raises her voice!
> On the hilltop along the road,
> she takes her stand at the crossroads.
> By the gates at the entrance to the town,
> on the road leading in, she cries aloud.
> (Proverbs 8:1-3, NLT)

See, the wisdom here isn't calling out to us when we've arrived in the town or made the decision about which way we're going. It's there as we're taking those steps, or when we're not sure about which step to take.

Let's just unpack the places where wisdom's calling out to us.

Wisdom along the road

Route 66 in America comes to mind. Though I've not yet driven along it, I can envisage a long, never-ending stretch of tarmac going through the desert. You can go for miles without encountering another person or town.

Haven't we all travelled roads like this in our lives? The pandemic situation felt like this. Time is moving forward, but it doesn't feel like there is an end in sight, or a route map to guide us. Just the long road we've been on and what looks like more ahead. All we can do is keep driving.

Wisdom at the crossroad junction

This is more of a standpoint. A place of action. You're at a decision point. Something has happened and you have a choice. Though there may be more choices than you were expecting!

I can think of lots of crossroad situations in my life, such as when I left my job and took voluntary redundancy. That surely was a crossroad junction. I had choices; I didn't have to leave. I could have moved into another role. However, I couldn't just stand still. I had to make that choice and then continue walking down that path I'd chosen.

Wisdom by the town's entrance gates

You've travelled the empty road without seeing anything. You've made those crossroad choices and, as the satnav would say, 'You have arrived at your destination.' Well, nearly. You're at the gates, those just-before moments, as you're heading into the place of change. The gates need to open for you to enter, or you could choose to turn around whether they open or not.

As you've been reading, you've probably thought of situations in your life that feel like one of these places. And it's when we think about these circumstances that we realise how central wisdom is at these times. I find it comforting to know that especially in the times when I need 'common sense', 'insight' and 'strength' the most, I have access to a source of help. What is this source? Are we talking about our own wisdom? The wisdom from friends and family? The wisdom of others we look up to?

No, what the Bible is talking about here is godly wisdom: 'From his mouth come knowledge and understanding' (Proverbs 2:6, NLT). That's the best kind you can get. The deluxe version. You just have to be willing to seek and listen to it! That isn't a flippant statement; we do need to ask for wisdom. Wisdom's calling out to us, shouting out for us to pay attention, but we need to answer.

When I was at the crossroads point, I needed His wisdom, the 'insight' so I could make the decision. When I made the decision to leave work, I was offered the opportunity to extend my notice period. Though I could have benefited financially, it didn't make sense with the other plans I had of going to

America. This was when I needed His 'insight', not mine. It was also asking for God's help, calling on that wisdom being offered to me, which enabled me to have 'common sense' and 'success' as I completed my work, to have 'strength' as I left my team and to not feel shaken by all the *people pleasing*, the *shoulds* and the *paralysing-keep-the-window-shut* thoughts that went through my mind.

Alongside wisdom, we need courage. But we are and we can be women of courage. We can face what we would have thought of as unimaginable and stand in the storm. We can drive along the never-ending road where nothing is familiar. We can take the leap at the crossroads into the next part of God's plan for us. Why?

Because look who's already way ahead, who knows every detail:

> Be strong. Take courage. Don't be intimidated. Don't give them a second thought because GOD, your God, is striding ahead of you. He's right there with you. He won't let you down; he won't leave you.
> (Deuteronomy 31:6, *The Message*)

We do need that tenacity, the determination and bravery we have in Him. Wherever we are in those places, we need His wisdom to take heart in knowing He's already gone ahead. He's been through all those grey areas. More importantly, though God's walked ahead, He's also choosing to walk with us, right by our side.

Leaving the ark

One month and twenty-six days had passed since Noah had removed the ark's roof and saw that the surface of the earth was drying. 'One year and ten days' had passed since they all entered the ark – God spoke to Noah:

On the twenty-seventh day of the second month the land was [entirely] dry. And God spoke to Noah, saying, 'Go out of the ark, you and your wife and your sons and their wives with you. Bring out with you every living thing from all flesh – birds and animals and every crawling thing that crawls on the earth – that they may breed abundantly on the earth, and be fruitful and multiply on the earth.' So Noah went out, and his wife and his sons and their wives with him [after being in the ark one year and ten days]. Every animal, every crawling thing, every bird – and whatever moves on the land – went out by families (types, groupings) from the ark. (Genesis 8:14-19)

This is another unexpected occurrence. They might have gone to sleep the night before, wondering when they would leave the ark, but *suddenly* God speaks on that twenty-seventh day. The reason why it's that day? Because the earth is completely dry. The ground is no longer soggy; not a trace of rain exists. Only now is the land finally ready for them. Only now is His judgement complete.

Can you imagine how Noah must have felt when God spoke to him? I think he would have been relieved, knowing that he had been obedient and God hadn't forgotten His promises to him. And then the realisation that they would be leaving the ark. His excitement to share the news with the family. I can picture him as he ran down the corridors, calling out, his voice raw with emotion. I hope they danced and praised God after the news had sunk in. The joy of their journey being over. All the animals they'd looked after had survived. Their provisions and planning had worked. They had not starved; there were still supplies left.

The reason why they left the ark 'one year and ten days' after they had boarded it was because God had remembered them months before, while those floodwaters raged over the earth. God 'made a wind blow over the land, and the waters receded' (Genesis 8:1). It was God's kindness that enabled the ark to come to rest among the peaks, the mountaintops to be seen, the window opened and the birds let out… until none of the floodwaters were left.

Unlike when they entered, there was no time warning. God didn't give them days to pack everything up. No. God said, 'Go out of the ark … So Noah went out'. Noah didn't debate. Every living thing on the ark left on that day.

Remember, when they had entered the ark, God closed the door behind them. This time the Bible doesn't say that God opened the door. I think Noah opened it because God didn't need to demonstrate that they were being protected against the flood. Instead, it was safe for Noah, his family and all the animals to step out of the ark and onto the post-flood earth.

So Noah pushed the door back and left, along with Emzara, Tia and Japheth, Sarah and Shem, Mert and Ham, with all of the animals following behind them. They were all greeted by the sight of the mountains surrounding them, clear skies and the smell of sun-warmed-soil. Did Emzara stop herself at the edge of the ark's walkway? No, I believe she would have courageously stepped out, the earth solid beneath her feet. Did Noah look behind him as they made their way down the mountain, at the ark resting against the peaks, amazed at how it had floated high over the waters and brought them to this new place?

The post-flood earth

Once they reached the ground, it's not surprising that the first thing Noah did was to build 'an altar to the Lord' (Genesis 8:20). He then took from the clean animals and birds (these would have included the doves, but not ravens) which had been brought onto the ark and made an offering:

> The LORD smelled the pleasing aroma [a soothing, satisfying scent] and the LORD said to Himself, 'I will never again curse the ground because of man, for the intent (strong inclination, desire) of man's heart is

wicked from his youth; and I will never again destroy
every living thing, as I have done.'
(Genesis 8:21)

Notice how the Lord reacts; the sacrifice smells pleasant to
Him. God has senses too. We are created in His image (Genesis
1:27). The first fragrance on the post-flood earth brought by
humans is a fragrance that satisfies the Lord. And what is the
Lord's response? He will 'never again curse the ground'. He will
'never again destroy every living thing' through a flood.

Noah and his family hadn't stepped onto a new planet.
Where the ark landed may not have been familiar to them, but
it was still the same earth they had lived on before. However, it
was a very different-looking post-flood earth.

The rain that fell on the earth wasn't a shower. It was
torrential rain on ground that had never experienced rain
before. And remember, 'all the fountains of the great deep
[subterranean waters] burst open, and the windows *and*
floodgates of the heavens were opened' (Genesis 7:11). It was a
tremendous amount of water with all its force. From above and
below this would have changed the shape of the earth, its
geography. There were new seas, oceans, lakes, rivers and
streams. And the very action of the floodwaters retreating
created changes too:

> So, it was mountains rising and valleys sinking that
> caused the floodwater to drain at the end of Noah's
> Flood. The water moved toward the low spots on the
> planet and the rising land was exposed. As a result of
> vertical movements in the earth's crust, the continents
> and mountains rose at the same time as the valleys and
> ocean floors sank.[37]

---

[37] Mike Oard, 'How did the waters of Noah's Flood drain off all the continents?'
Creation Ministries International, online article sourced from *Creation* magazine,
Volume 37, Issue 3, July 2015, pp 28-30, creation.com/how-did-the-waters-of-

When we read Psalm 104, there are some familiar flood-related words in its verses:[38]

> You covered it with the deep as with a garment;
> The waters were standing above the mountains.
> At Your rebuke they fled;
> At the sound of Your thunder they hurried away.
> *The mountains rose, the valleys sank down.*
> To the place which You established for them.
> You set a boundary [for the waters] that they may not cross over,
> So that they will not return to cover the earth.
> (Psalm 104:6-9, italics mine)

There is clear evidence in geomorphology about the worldwide impact of the flood on the earth with how the mountains and valleys moved. [39] Noah and his family now stood on this changed ground, along with all the animals. This was going to be a world where every day the sky wouldn't be blue. The sun wouldn't always shine. Grey clouds would gather. How would they not be scared a flood wasn't going to happen each time the rain drops fell?

God anticipated how they would feel. He gave Noah and his family reassurance about the patterns of weather. They wouldn't need to fear a flood that would destroy the entire earth again. God said to them:

noahs-flood-drain (accessed 23rd October 2020). Permission given from Creation Ministries International.

[38] Charles Taylor, 'Did mountains really rise according to Psalm 104:8?', Creation Ministries International, online article sourced from *Journal of Creation* 12, Issue 3, 1998, pp 312-313, creation.com/images/pdfs/tj/j12_3/j12_3_312-313.pdf; 'Charles Taylor replies', Creation Ministries International, online article sourced from *Journal of Creation*, 13, Issue 1, 1999, pp 70-71, creation.com/images/pdfs/tj/j13_1/j13_1_68-71.pdf (both accessed 23rd October 2020). Permission given from Creation Ministries International.

[39] Mike Oard, 'How did the waters of Noah's Flood drain off all the continents?' Permission given from Creation Ministries International.

> While the earth remains,
> Seedtime and harvest,
> Cold and heat,
> Winter and summer,
> And day and night
> Shall not cease.
> (Genesis 8:22)

This is the world we live in today. There are many voices that speak of the negative impact humanity has on the planet and how this is subsequently affecting the earth. But here in the Word of God is His promise about His world (Psalm 24:1). We don't need to invest all our time trying to solve or stop it. And since that time when He first spoke these words, we have had 'day and night'; we have had 'Winter and summer'; we have had times when crops grow and times when we pick them, and we will continue to do so 'While the earth remains'.

His rainbow

Just like Noah had to have faith when God told him about the flood, he and his family had to trust that the whole earth would not flood again and what God had promised would endure:

> Then God spoke to Noah and to his sons with him, saying, 'Now behold, I am establishing My covenant (binding agreement, solemn promise) with you and with your descendants after you and with every living creature that is with you – the birds, the livestock, and the wild animals of the earth along with you, of everything that comes out of the ark – every living creature of the earth. I will establish My covenant with you: Never again shall all flesh be cut off by the water of a flood, nor shall there ever again be a flood to destroy *and* ruin the earth.'
> (Genesis 9:8-11)

The first time a covenant is mentioned in the Bible is when God gave His 'solemn promise' to Noah that he and his family would enter the ark (Genesis 6:18). Here we have God again in Genesis 9 giving a binding agreement to Noah, his family, all the animals and their 'descendants', so that means it applies even to *us*. God cares about His creation, from the beetle to the bear, the gerbil to the giraffe.

God didn't just tell them, though. Don't you love that about Him? God's been through the pain and grief of witnessing the sin and lawlessness of the pre-flood earth, watched Noah build the ark yet restrained His judgement, then sent the rain and destroyed all the life that remained, and now He was speaking these promises to the earth. The promise that was for Emzara is relevant for us now. And in addition to those words, God gave a sign, and a beautiful one. Do you think this has something to do with a rainbow?

> And God said, 'This is the token (visible symbol, memorial) of the [solemn] covenant which I am making between Me and you and every living creature that is with you, for all future generations; I set My rainbow in the clouds, and it shall be a sign of a covenant between Me and the earth.'
> (Genesis 9:12-13)

Picture the sight. Tia had stepped out of the ark they'd lived on for a year and ten days. She was now having to become accustomed to being outside, to the space of the land around her, after having been confined in the ark. She was just trying to handle her emotions when suddenly the sky, which had been clear and blue, clouded over. Grey covered it. This was how the sky looked when they had entered the ark. Tia might have been scared; she knew there wasn't going to be another flood like the earth had just experienced, but...

However, the sun hadn't completely disappeared; its rays still shone from behind her. Then in front of her appeared a beautiful band of bright colours like nothing she had seen before. The banner arced across the sky, cutting through the clouds.

None of the people or animals had ever seen such a sight; they would have been unable to describe it. So God told them what the banner was: 'My rainbow'. 'My', that's a possessive pronoun – the rainbow is His. And what does God promise He'll do every time there is a rainbow in the sky?

> It shall come about, when I bring clouds over the earth, that the rainbow shall be seen in the clouds, and I will [compassionately] remember My covenant, which is between Me and you and every living creature of all flesh; and never again will the water become a flood to destroy all flesh. When the rainbow is in the clouds and I look at it, I will [solemnly] remember the everlasting covenant between God and every living creature of all flesh that is on the earth.
> (Genesis 9:14-16)

God remembers when there is a rainbow in the sky.

He remembers His covenant He made with us, with the bees, beetles and bears, with every living thing. All the times since the first rainbow, whenever that arch appears, He remembers.

We love looking at rainbows, don't we?

We may remember when we see them about God's promise after the flood, but next time you see a rainbow, remember that God is remembering His promise too. God is recalling the day when He made a rainbow appear for the first time.

You might have sung the song as a child, like I did, about all their colours.[40] We can identify what those seven colours are when we see a rainbow, again that repeat of the holy number seven. But there may be a whole multitude of tones that we can't

---

[40] Arthur Hamilton, born 22nd October 1926, 'Sing a Rainbow', https://www.songfacts.com/facts/arthur-hamilton/sing-a-rainbow (accessed 23rd October 2020).

see with our eyes.[41] Perhaps, when God created the rainbow, He used all the colours of His creation. We know He loves colours. Something to add to the list of questions I'll ask Him in heaven!

What's also incredible about rainbows is that, though we see it as an arch in the sky, the rainbow is actually a complete circle.[42] We're not able to view the entire shape of the rainbow at the ground level, but there are times when you're in an aircraft that you're able to see the actual circle.[43] So just think, whenever God sees a rainbow, He's seeing the shape of the earth. His banner of love encircling it (Song of Solomon 2:4).

Rainbows as a symbol

The rainbow made a noteworthy impression on Noah and his family. Since the first time God placed it in the sky, that impression has carried on through the generations and the rainbow has become a symbol. Even now for us in the twenty-first century, rainbows epitomise hope, and surely that's part of what God wanted the rainbow to give? They are seen many times across different creative interpretations and civilisations, symbolising the expectation of greater days ahead.[44]

I feel joyful when I see a rainbow. There is something so special about seeing the colours radiating in the sky. We don't get to see rainbows all the time, and when we do see one, we

[41] 'What are the colours of the rainbow?', Met Office, www.metoffice.gov.uk/weather/learn-about/weather/optical-effects/rainbows/colours-of-the-rainbow. Contains public sector information licensed under the Open Government Licence v3.0, www.nationalarchives.gov.uk/doc/open-government-licence/version/3/ (accessed 23rd October 2020).

[42] 'Why rainbows are curved', *EarthSky*, 9th April 2018, earthsky.org/earth/what-gives-rainbows-their-curved-shape (accessed 23rd October 2020).

[43] Ibid.

[44] Gaia Vince, 'Rainbows as signs of thank you, hope and solidarity', BBC Culture, 9th April 2020, www.bbc.com/culture/article/20200409-rainbows-as-signs-of-thank-you-hope-and-solidarity (accessed 23rd October 2020).

react to the sight. We can't stop ourselves from pointing it out to others: 'Look, there's a rainbow!' Rainbows fill us with an emotion.

When we see a rainbow, we may recollect the ark story, although some people may be unaware of its meaning, and for others it could be a mystical sign. These kinds of associations draw us away from the truth of what the rainbow really represents. It isn't surprising that the enemy wants to divert our attention away from its Creator.

The message of hope we have in rainbows was very much around me during the pandemic. I was surrounded by their bright colours, not in the sky, but on posters stuck on windows; chalk drawings made on pavements and walls; on clothes; banners; food; advertising and social media. The rainbow across countries became a key symbol throughout the pandemic. A drawing that made us smile. A symbol to show our thankfulness for those who worked in the healthcare and front-line sectors. The rainbow had been so widely used within the early months of the pandemic that it was referred to in a televised speech made by Her Majesty the Queen in April 2020:

> The moments when the United Kingdom has come together to applaud its care and essential workers will be remembered as an expression of our national spirit; and its symbol will be the rainbows drawn by children.[45]

Why were we drawn to the rainbow as a symbol at that time?

There may be a surface level reason why people in the pandemic chose it, but I think it is because of this deeper meaning that rainbows have. The covenant promise made by God. We can link the rainbow symbol right back to His heart

---

[45] Her Majesty the Queen, 'The Queen's Broadcast to the UK and Commonwealth', The Royal Household, 5th April 2020, www.royal.uk/queens-broadcast-uk-and-commonwealth. Contains public sector information licensed under the Open Government Licence v3.0, www.nationalarchives.gov.uk/doc/open-government-licence/version/3/ (accessed 23rd October 2020).

and the resounding message behind it of His love and faithfulness to us.

God's faithfulness

The rainbow disappeared from the sky. Imagine Emzara, Tia, Sarah and Mert as they looked around and felt that familiar feeling of day one on the ark, coupled with the sense that there was even more to do this time. They'd left the ark but there wasn't a row of ready-made structures Noah had built for them. They'd need to establish their homes, work the ground. All the plans they'd made would have to be achieved, and new plans too. More unanswered questions must have gone through their minds as they talked with the men about where to set up their tents, as they lit the first fire and prepared their first meal.

I'd like to think they sat outside, not wanting to be under any cover after all the time inside the ark, watching instead the sunset colours streak across the sky, then the stars twinkling and the moonlight.

God's faithfulness surrounded them. His faithfulness surrounds us now.

The rainbow reminds us that God remembers. But it also speaks of His faithfulness, majesty and glory. When the prophet Ezekiel in the Old Testament had the vision of the throne, he described the appearance of a man seated on it:

> *There was* a brightness *and* a remarkable radiance [like a halo] around Him. As the appearance of the rainbow in the clouds on a rainy day, so was the appearance of the surrounding radiance. This was the appearance of the likeness of the glory *and* brilliance of the LORD.
> (Ezekiel 1:27-28)

Ezekiel compared God's glory to being like a rainbow, the radiance surrounding Him like those rainbow colours. John also used a rainbow to make the comparison when he saw God's throne in heaven: 'encircling the throne *there* was a rainbow that looked like [the color of an] emerald' (Revelation 4:3). Isn't it absolutely incredible to think these rainbow colours are in heaven?

God chose to use His heavenly colours, the colours encircling His throne, to be the sign of His covenant when they encircled the earth after the flood. Not only was God saying this is 'My rainbow' (Genesis 9:13), but it's part of His throne, of who He is. After everything God had to do with the flood, I think He gave this sign to say it's still 'My earth'. And He didn't just show the rainbow to Noah and his family as a one-off special. He continues to show their descendants. Each time we see a rainbow we're getting a glimpse into the heavenly throne room of God. I think that's why rainbows fill us with such joy.

We don't need to wait to see a rainbow in a stormy sky to know God loves us each day. Though the world chooses to use it as a symbol of hope, we have an even greater understanding about the heart of the rainbow's creator. We call Him 'Abba! Father!' (Romans 8:15). We know the depth, height, length and breadth of God's love for us (Ephesians 3:18).

When you can't feel His love, when the enemy whispers that God doesn't love you, remember the rainbow. As Genesis 9:15 tells us, God compassionately remembers His covenant. Compassion is a strong emotion, full of tenderness, concern and care:

> 'But with everlasting kindness I will have compassion on you,'
> Says the LORD your Redeemer.
> 'For this is *like* the waters of Noah to Me,
> As I swore [an oath] that the waters of Noah
> Would not flood the earth again;
> In the same way I have sworn that I will not be angry with you
> Nor will I rebuke you.
> For the mountains may be removed and the hills may shake,
> But My lovingkindness will not be removed from you,

Nor will My covenant of peace be shaken,'
Says the LORD who has compassion on you.
(Isaiah 54:8-10)

God is faithful. God remembers us. God's compassion for us is infinite.

Father, thank You for being such a wise and gracious Father. That You want to help me when I need help the most in those unknown places. When I read about the rainbow, I want to praise You. As Moses said, 'Ascribe greatness and honor to our God. The Rock! His work is perfect, For all His ways are just; A God of faithfulness without iniquity ... Just and upright [are You]. [46] *You kept Your promise to Noah that the flood would end and his family would be safe. You then gave us a promise which remains to this day, and with this promise You showed us Your glory, the majesty of Your throne. Help me to remember the rainbow's true message, to keep Your promises in my heart and to trust in Your love.*
Amen.

---

[46] Deuteronomy 32:3-4, with author additions in brackets.

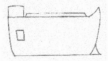

Chapter contemplations

- Read Deuteronomy 31:6 and meditate on it. Write the verse out, keep it in your purse, memorise and remember it for those times you feel wobbly. Take courage – God is way ahead of where you are.

- Consider the Genesis flood chapters. Have your thoughts changed so far about the ark story? How?

- Pray that God will open up an opportunity for you to have a conversation with someone about the meaning of a rainbow so you can share His love with them.

Journal pages

9

The Mothers of Many

At the start of Genesis 9, the Lord blessed Noah and his family and established the new principles for the post-flood earth. Up until this point there had been no grandchildren, but here God spoke about the earth being filled with people (Genesis 9:1). It wasn't just Tia, Sarah and Mert who would give birth, but so would the animals who had left the ark. Soon again baby lambs would leap, calves would suckle and chirping chicks would follow their parents. 'As for you, be fruitful and multiply; Populate the earth abundantly and multiply in it' (Genesis 9:7).

Noah's descendants

We know Noah was descended from Seth, Adam and Eve's third son. And we learn from Genesis 9 that though our genealogy traces right back to Adam and Eve, we are also all descended from Noah. We either come from Japheth, Shem or Ham; it was, 'from these [men] *[and women]* the whole earth was populated *and* scattered with inhabitants' (Genesis 9:19).[47]

Imagine the birth of the first baby. There was no hospital, no midwife or doctors on call. Emzara didn't wait at a distance to hold her first grandchildren. No, I think she was there in the tent, remembering what her mother and grandmother had taught her, helping Tia, till the final contraction, the second of

---

[47] Author's addition in italicised square brackets.

silence while everyone inside and out held their breath. Then the piercing cry of a newborn. Imagine Emzara's relief as Tia nursed her son. More labours, more newborn cries, as brothers and sisters were born.

How the families scattered

Genesis 10 is known as the Table of Nations because it gives us information about the descendants of Noah through his three sons and daughters-in-law. Japheth had seven sons, Shem had five sons and Ham had four sons (Genesis 10:2, 22, 6), though they indeed may have had more sons, and the records don't include their daughters, or any children that were lost. The chapter clearly shows they were fruitful; they did multiply and spread out across the earth. We know from the Bible the ark landed on the mountains of Ararat (Genesis 8:4), which is in eastern Turkey, close to the borders with Armenia, Iran and the Nakhchivan enclave of Azerbaijan. It was from this point that the families would have eventually spread out into the land.

Genesis 10:5 says that Japheth's children were '[the people of] the coastlands'. The sea was in Japheth's blood and his children travelled across it, and 'went Northward, and settled in regions around the Black and Caspian Seas' and were the forerunners of the people in 'Europe and Asia'.[48] When we look at some of Shem's children's names, we can tell they went into Persia, Syria and Mesopotamia (Elam, Aram and Asshur), whereas Ham's children went more towards the south into Africa and along its eastern coast.[49] The Egyptians were descended from Ham's son, Mizraim (Genesis 10:6). Is that why the pyramids were built so well and still exist today? Noah's construction skills passed down through his line.

---

[48] Taken from *Halley's Bible Handbook* by Dr Henry H Halley Copyright © 1965 by Dr Henry H Halley. Used by permission of Zondervan, www.zondervan.com, p 81.
[49] 'Shem, Ham and Japheth', Bible History, www.bible-history.com/old-testament/desc-shem-ham-japheth.html (accessed 23rd October 2020).

God clearly wants us to know where we came from. In Genesis 1, He tells us how we were created by Him, and then in Genesis 10, He gives us through these records the history of our post-flood generational history. We're not from monkeys; we're not from some microscopic particle of millennia-old amoeba: which are lies Satan wants the world to believe, thereby distracting us from knowing our Creator. We're the amazing, hand-crafted and bespoke children of God. And after the flood, as Adam's descendants left the ark, God again reinforced this to us:

> These are the families of the sons of Noah, according to their descendants, by their nations; and from these [people] the nations were separated *and* spread abroad on the earth after the flood.
> (Genesis 10:32)

All these families wouldn't have grown and 'separated' if it hadn't been for Noah's son's wives. If Tia didn't nurture her firstborn, Gomer. If Sarah hadn't brought up little Elam. If Mert hadn't looked after Cush. These babies didn't just pop out and multiply; they had to be mothered. These children, grandchildren, great-grandchildren, great-great-grandchildren, great-great-great-grandchildren and beyond. All of them related to Tia, Sarah and Mert. They are indeed the mothers of many.

Generational lines

The role of these three women expanded as they all learned about parenthood. Meals still had to prepared, households managed, clothes made, washing done, plants watered, animals fed and children looked after.

The women didn't have our modern-day society, with all its comforts, but strip these back and we are just like them. Besides physical characteristics, think of the skills Tia, Sarah and Mert instilled into their daughters and then how these were passed on. We're not talking only about homemaking skills here. Yes,

Sarah might have taught her daughters how to make a good flatbread! But there is so much to each one of us. We are multifaceted. What similarities do we share with the wives of Noah's sons?

We know that health issues, and good or bad characteristics can be passed down through family lines. We're asked by doctors, 'Is anyone in your family diabetic? Is there a history of heart disease?' How many times have we been at family gatherings and a relative has said, 'Aren't you tall, just like your father,' or, 'You worry too much, you're like your grandmother.' There are families who share artistic or creative talents.

As I've learned more about my family line, I've been able to trace similarities. I think some of my business ability stems from my great-great-grandmother (on my mum's side) who in the early twentieth century developed and managed a launderette business in the town where she lived. She built houses for her workers and even a church in 1912 so they didn't need to have services in the main launderette. That's quite something for a woman of her time. I got to know more about my dad's line, especially from my trip to America in 2018, so I can see where my love of dancing (not professionally!), homemaking and people skills come from. And then other traits from my mum's line, as well as traits that cut across both. They all intertwine and are linked together with the unique talents and abilities God had planned just for me.

Though I'm able to understand the good that has come down my generational lines, I've also discerned the not so good: the lines of fear and anxiety and specific generational sins that have needed to be broken. In Deuteronomy 5:9 God talks about ancestral sin that passes on 'to the third and ... fourth *generations*'. We know Jesus dying on the cross took all these sins and more from us (John 19:30), but sometimes we need to make that deliberate act of breaking past sins and asking God for healing to come into our lives. I've definitely noticed the change after I've prayed about those issues and seen how fears have disappeared.

Our walk with God is a daily one. We are being changed from 'glory to … glory' (2 Corinthians 3:18). We will never be perfect (praise the Lord!) until we're transformed into our renewed bodies. God shows:

> graciousness *and* lovingkindness to thousands [of generations] of those who love *[Him]* and keep *[His]* commandments.
> (Deuteronomy 5:10)[50]

He cares deeply for us and wants us to be whole. As we go through our lives He will reveal, like the layers of the onion I've talked about before, the things that may hold us back or bind us up, whether we don't know or do know about them. God wants us to be free and to live in the freedom Jesus bought for us at the cross. God doesn't want us giving any footholds to the enemy.

Understanding where we come from and how we fit, matters. We see this in the ancestry programmes and ancestral tree searches people make. We want to know whether we have a royal connection; if our ancestors travelled over from distant lands; what they did for work, and whether this has any links to us. This search is all about the pursuit of being able to place ourselves.

Family is important to God

Whether we love our family, like our family, get on with our family, or even know our family, family is important to God.

If God didn't believe in family, then why did He save one?

God didn't have to save Noah. He could have just flooded the earth and created people again, or He could have saved only Noah, and then when the ark door opened, a new wife could have been there waiting outside for him, holding up a welcome

---

[50] Author's addition in italicised square brackets.

sign. But no, God didn't choose any of those options. Because of Noah's righteousness, he *and his family* were saved.

Along with being part of a family come all of those family dynamics. The disagreements we have, the harsh words that can be spoken and turned into feuds; as Jesus said, 'a family splintered by feuding will fall apart' (Mark 3:25, NLT). Besides wholeness in families, there can be divisions. There is a breadth of hurt and pain that can come from how family members act towards each other. God didn't intend for families to be broken or for relatives to hurt and harm us. Satan knows the suffering that can be caused through people. We know the enemy is out to rob anything he can (John 10:10), to cast darkness over our families, to bring shadows into our relationships, to weigh us down with the emotions of bitterness and resentment caused by what they do. And the enemy's destruction and the way people behave can be seen across the years and generations.

You will have your own story about family. It's increasingly rare in these times to have had a stable, loving upbringing from both parents, but you might have been blessed with this. The word 'family' for you, though, may cause pain because you're estranged from your relatives or have not had that family experience. You could have been lovingly embraced and adopted into a family, or perhaps your childhood was a series of foster placements where nowhere ever felt like home.

My family has had its ups and downs. I was raised by my mum after my parents had to separate. I've lived in the same town as my grandparents since I was a young child, so was able to see them regularly until they passed away only recently, but this doesn't mean it was all wonderful. Because of my health problems as a child, I was home-schooled from the age of seven until nineteen. It was amazing how the Lord opened the doors so Mum could stay at home with me and the schooling system allowed it. This was back in the days when home-schooling was frowned upon in the UK, not a common global word like it has become. Because of the issues my dad had, and with what had happened in my parents' relationship, it was only really after his death in 2002 that I was able to start building some connections with relatives on his side. Those connections really took on meaning and became more personal when God brought about the trip to the States in 2018.

I have seen God's care in restoring family in my life, as slowly, softly there has been healing, and there is more to be done. I have relatives on both sides of the pond who I'm still getting to know. We may not see each other much, but we know we're family. And for me, I feel more whole in knowing who my family are and in having those connections restored.

Of course, it doesn't mean everything is perfect – are families ever? Like with any relationship we have, it's God's love that enables us to forgive, and to continue with an attitude of forgiveness and grace that only He can supply. Whether your family is literally separated and broken apart, or you're hurting from the wounds they've caused, wherever you are in your family situation, then bring it to Him, because He is the God who restores. He has a compassionate heart. He'll 'pick up the pieces from all the places where you were scattered' (Deuteronomy 30:4, *The Message*). He is the God who makes us 'whole' (1 Thessalonians 5:23), even if we're unable to have the wholeness we may want in our families.

God's family is important to Him

Whatever is going on with our worldly family, we must remember we're also in a family on another entirely different level. When we give our lives to God, and believe Jesus died on the cross for us, we become part of His family. We're adopted as His 'children through Jesus Christ, in accordance with the kind intention *and* good pleasure of His will' (Ephesians 1:5). God always wanted this level of connection and intimacy with us. He wants us to call Him 'Abba! Father!' (Romans 8:15). That's why He gave His only Son for us, so that through Jesus' death, our relationship with Him could be restored.

If you want to know whether you have royal blood in your lines from your ancestors, it doesn't matter. Why? Because He is 'KING OF KINGS, AND LORD OF LORDS' (Revelation 19:16), so we have the best royal connections possible! God doesn't just adopt us, but wholeheartedly welcomes us and treats us as such, so we also become part of His 'royal PRIESTHOOD' (1 Peter 2:9).

Being part of God's family also means we join the body of Christ, otherwise known as the Church (1 Corinthians 12:27-28). Many of us will have experienced the fellowship that comes through being with our brothers and sisters in Him. I had men and women who were like family to me while I was growing up. The Lord used them to help fill the gaps He knew were missing.

But just like with any human interaction, there can be issues too. We don't shake off our weaknesses when we join the Church family. Brokenness and need present themselves; people hurt each other. We can't expect everyone to be faultless because we're not in our own homes. Jesus realises this, and there are so many scriptures about His Church. In 1 Corinthians 12:12-26, Paul speaks about the body of Christ, all the various parts it comprises and how we're all connected through our faith in Him, but I think what's crucial is the next chapter, which is about love. Ultimately, this is what we need for each other in the family of God, and for His love to help us when we go through those difficult times, like in any family.

The body of Christ is bigger, though, than the church we choose to attend. The Church is the body of believers across the world. This was especially emphasised during the pandemic, as congregations learned to be creative and make services available online. Believers have been able to come together from various countries. We don't need to be in a building to connect; we can virtually encourage one another and experience that wider bond beyond the local church. Knowing we're part of the bigger world family of God is really important.

Friendship is important to God

There are many different types of friendship we experience: some friends walk with us for a short time; others know us

170

throughout our lives; and there are those who're like extended family to us.

God isn't ignorant of friendship. He made Adam and Eve so they would have companionship with each other. He knew it wasn't good for us to be alone (Genesis 2:18). We've already spoken about how they walked with God in the Garden of Eden, and how Noah walked with the Lord. That action of walking is intimate; it's active. My friends know that I love to go for a walk and talk with them. There's something so special about spending time together like that, as your feet pick up pace with your conversation, or when you can just quietly sit and look at a view – and with me, a coffee stop somewhere has to be involved too. It was hard during the pandemic not to see family or friends in the same way as I did before.

We missed having that closeness with people; we needed those connections, whether a long catch-up chat or a casual conversation. Though technology allowed us to remain in touch, seeing friends on a screen isn't quite the same. I think we learned about how we still need to actually see people in the flesh.

The pandemic for some people brought a deeper sense of isolation and loneliness. Yet we know there are many who experience seclusion as part of their everyday lives; for them it isn't a result of an unprecedented event.

Perhaps some of us used the time to reconsider how we can be a friend to those around us who need one.

Friends can bring so many layers into our lives. What can sound hurtful when a family member harshly blurts out advice can be taken differently from a friend; it doesn't have the same impact. As Proverbs 27:6 says, 'Faithful are the wounds of a friend [who corrects out of love and concern]', and we need those people we can trust, whose advice we can consider and be able to talk things through with. It's good to be able to carry each other's loads (Galatians 6:2), and having those kinds of trusted friendships is so precious, where we can be ourselves and feel safe.

Jesus had friends. He didn't go through His ministry time alone. He had disciples who supported Him, they travelled and ate meals together. They were the ones who were given 'The mystery of the kingdom of God'; they had 'teachable hearts' (Mark 4:11). Jesus also chose twelve of them from the disciples, whom He called 'apostles' (Luke 6:13-16). You could say they were His inner circle, but again, like with any relationship, they had problems. There were times when they squabbled about who was most important to Jesus (Luke 9:46), Judas betrayed Him (Mark 14:10), and when Jesus was arrested, Peter denied ever knowing Him, even though he had earlier told Jesus he would never do such a thing (Mark 14:29-31, 66-72).

It's hard when in our friendships we let each other down. We have expectations about behaviour, and sometimes what we say, or what our friends say to us, doesn't come from the place of love and concern Proverbs 27:6 mentions. When we need our friends in the valley seasons of our lives, we often find that they don't know how to act or speak to us. We can find it hard to be the kind of friend we think people need us to be in those times too. Sometimes that's when friendships can fracture.

Jesus was going through a difficult time when He went into the Garden of Gethsemane ahead of what He knew was coming at the cross. He was with His especially close group of twelve disciples, and He told them to wait while He moved away to pray (Mark 14:32):

> He took Peter, James, and John with him, and he became deeply troubled and distressed. He told them, 'My soul is crushed with grief to the point of death. Stay here and keep watch with me.'
> (Mark 14:33-34, NLT)

Jesus moved a little further away and prayed; after an hour, he went back to His friends. I think He humanly needed their comfort, knowing they were keeping watch for Him, but instead He found them sleeping. He went back to pray, and then returned to them; again they were asleep. And again they couldn't answer why they couldn't stay awake: 'they did not know how to answer Him' (Mark 14:35-40).

In our humanity we make so many mistakes that affect all areas of our lives, including our relationships. *We may not know what to say.* Despite them being apostles and Jesus' friends, Peter, James and John were unable to support Him, even though Jesus asked them to. And as Jesus said when He found them asleep, 'Keep watch and pray, so that you will not give in to temptation. For the spirit is willing, but the body is weak' (Mark 14:38, NLT). Though the wider context of this verse can be taken in reference to praying, Jesus also points out the weakness of our flesh; the inability of our body to always do what we might want it to. And that includes how we behave with our friends. Sometimes, though, it may not be our intent; we will let them down and find they let us down too.

That's where forgiveness steps in; we can forgive because Jesus first forgave us (Ephesians 4:32). Though we may not be able to forget what people do, be they friends or family, when we forgive, it releases the power of the emotions we feel about what they've done; the bitterness and anger that are only going to hurt us. Forgiveness doesn't mean we excuse their actions or behaviour. It may be hard for us humanly to contemplate forgiving someone who's badly hurt us or a loved one; this is when we need to call on the help from our Father. He is the One who will help us to forgive when we ask Him to, because He is all about forgiveness; He removes our sins 'As far as the east is from the west' (Psalm 103:12), and when He forgives us He doesn't recollect or dwell on what we've done wrong (Hebrews 8:12).

Jesus spoke about friendship with His disciples when He said, 'No one has greater love [nor stronger commitment] than to lay down his own life for his friends' (John 15:13). There is a stronger message here than the attitude we're to have with friends, and in itself, that's quite an attitude to sacrifice your life for others. But Jesus also tells us here how He thinks of us: as His friends, because *He died for us.*

I think it's so powerful that Jesus was beaten, tortured, pierced and killed for me *because He thinks of me as His friend.* He loved me that much. He loves us that much whether we view Him as our friend or not.

Jesus didn't die to earn the best friend badge. He died so that we would be free of the fallen nature of sin that had come into the world. Jesus died so that when we're judged, we're found clean and righteous in Him because He took all our sin (Revelation 20:12; 2 Corinthians 5:21). He hung there on the cross willingly so I could live eternally. He is one absolutely amazing friend, and I love Him so much for the freedom I have through believing in Him.

Irrespective of how many friends we have, we will never, ever lose the friendship we have with Jesus. He is always ready to walk and talk with us, and to help us walk and talk in His love (2 John 1:6).

Father, thank You so much for Jesus, for sending Your Son to save me. Thank You for embracing me into Your family, that You see me as Yours, and I can come to You as my Abba Father. You are everything I need. Though I may not know all my family history, who my ancestors are, thank You that they contributed to me being on the earth today. I know You care about family and I want to pray for mine. You know what's going on with my circumstances. You know the issues I face and the healing my family needs. I ask for restoration and wholeness in my family. Help me with my friendships, Jesus, to learn from Your example, and mostly to act out of love in all my relationships. When I find it hard to know what to say, please help me.
Amen.

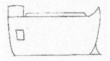

Chapter contemplations

- Read through Genesis 10 to help you understand more about some of Noah's descendants.

- Spend some time with the Lord reflecting on your family and friendships; note your thoughts in your journal.

- Go for a walk and talk with a friend. There doesn't need to be a reason – just spend time enjoying being with them and having fun together.

Journal pages

10
After the Flood

When Noah's daughters-in-law left the ark, they entered into a new stage of their journey, knowing they would bear children and become mothers. As well as handling this news, Noah and his family were presented with other post-flood changes by God. The ark hadn't returned to where Noah had first built it, and neither was the family going to return to how life was before the flood.

So, what were those after-the-flood changes? We've spoken already about some of what God said in Genesis 9, and now we're going to explore some other aspects. One of the new post-flood earth principles God established was our relationship with food.

Food is important to God

In the previous chapter we talked about the importance of family and friendship to God. There is also a link here between them and food.

Being with others and eating around a table brings a lot of pleasure and fun. There are those moments when everyone reaches to take the last spoonful of roast potatoes, or can't wait to tuck into a piece of Mum's famous lemon meringue pie. The pleasure we take in eating together goes beyond family; whether we're enjoying dishes we've prepared with friends or sharing a table with strangers, food brings us together.

Food is mentioned throughout the Bible, which I'm pleased about, because I love food. And there are many women, and men, like me who take delight in preparing food and feeding people. I think God understands the comfort and nourishment food brings to us. After all, God knew it was important enough to instruct Noah to make sure they collected and stored enough food for them and the animals. And we've got these two strands we can see from the flood about food: how we react to food and the pleasure it brings, with how God sees food. God cared for and retained Noah's family unit, and God cared that they had enough food.

If we take the first and last books in the Bible, we can see the focus on food from beginning to end, with Genesis 1:11 talking of the land sprouting vegetation to eat in the Garden of Eden to the Tree of Life in Revelation 22:2, which bears twelve different kinds of produce and provides 'its fruit every month'. Jesus' miracles included food. His first miracle was turning water into a vintage wine for a wedding feast (John 2:1-11). When Jesus spoke, He cared for the crowds, and masses were fed through just five loaves and two fish – and not just enough to fill a gap until they got home. The five loaves and two fish were multiplied so that there were many basketfuls left over (John 6:1-14). Then, after Jesus died at the cross and was resurrected, He appeared to His disciples. One of the ways He showed it was really Him in bodily form was by eating some fish (Luke 24:40-43). I find it very reassuring to know that, even with Jesus' heavenly body, He could still eat.

It shouldn't be a surprise to see food throughout the Bible. God made us. He knows we need to eat. Not just to eat for strength, but He made us with tastebuds so we could enjoy the flavours of the various foods He created too.

After the flood, though, we see a difference in how God views food, with new guidance for Noah and his family about their relationship with it:

> Every moving thing that lives shall be food for you; I
> give you everything, as *I gave* you the green plants *and*
> vegetables. But you shall not eat meat along with its life,
> *that is*, its blood.
> (Genesis 9:3-4)

Though the earth was still the same earth God created right at
the start, He was making changes. The Garden of Eden was no
longer visible. The geography was different. Now as Tia looked
at the rabbits hopping along on the ground, God said she
could eat them. But we don't know if she chose to! God was
establishing a totally new relationship with what they ate; now
He tells them, 'Every moving thing that lives shall be food for
you.' I wonder how Emzara, Tia, Sarah and Mert felt, being told
they could now eat lambs and chickens? The taste of meat
would be unusual for them, but from this point they could
choose to eat it when they wouldn't have before.

When the earth was first created, God said to Adam and Eve:

> Behold, I have given you every plant yielding seed that
> is on the surface of the entire earth, and every tree which
> has fruit yielding seed; it shall be food for you; and to all
> the animals on the earth and to every bird of the air and
> to everything that moves on the ground – to everything
> in which there is the breath of life – *I have given* every
> green plant for food.
> (Genesis 1:29-30)

So this means up until the flood it is highly unlikely that humans
ate animals, animals ate humans, or animals ate each other.
Food at that time for everyone came from plants and trees.
Nothing was carnivorous. Yes, they may have killed lambs as an
act of sacrifice, but this doesn't mean that they ate them.[51] We
know when Adam and Eve first became aware they were naked,
God made them coverings of animal skin (Genesis 3:21), and

---

[51] Rice, *In the Beginning*, p 232.

that Abel had 'flocks [of sheep and goats]' (Genesis 4:2). But it's likely these were kept for offerings or perhaps to be used for garments.

However, I don't think Noah and his family would have even contemplated eating meat before this point. What God spoke to Adam and Eve in the garden would have been passed down from them to Seth and so on. God doesn't make any further statement about what to eat after Genesis 1 until Genesis 9, which is when Noah and his family leave the ark. The next time God speaks at length about food in the Old Testament is in Leviticus and Deuteronomy,[52] where God instructs Moses and Aaron in regard to food for the Jewish people.

Animals are important to God

Alongside the change about what they could now all eat, there was a change in their relationships with animals. Perhaps this was why before God talked about eating every moving thing in Genesis 9:3, He said:

> The fear and the terror of you shall be [instinctive] in every animal of the land and in every bird of the air; and together with everything that moves on the ground, and with all the fish of the sea; they are given into your hand. (Genesis 9:2)

Before the flood the animals wouldn't have been scared of humans. Now they were, maybe because they had become aware humans could eat them. And they also instinctively knew they could eat each other. This was the first time a lion became a carnivore; before then lions might have preferred carrots.

Genesis 9 has very strong similarities to the blessing God gave to Adam and Eve in Genesis 1 after the earth was created.

---

[52] Such as Leviticus 11:1-12; Deuteronomy 14:3-21. Before this, in Exodus 12, food is also mentioned in context to the Passover Lamb and Feast of Unleavened Bread.

God was telling Noah and his family to be fruitful and multiply, what their relationship with animals would be and what they were to eat, just like He did with Adam and Eve:

> Be fruitful and multiply. Fill the earth and govern it.
> Reign over the fish in the sea, the birds in the sky, and
> all the animals that scurry along the ground.
> (Genesis 1:28, NLT)

The animals Adam and Eve knew weren't afraid of them, though. Neither did Noah have to struggle with looking after the bison, nor was he scared of the snakes on the ark. No, Noah had dominion over every living thing, just like everyone else who lived up until the flood. And now in Genesis 9, a sharp contrast was introduced because humankind no longer had control over all the animals. Our interaction with them changed. Think about our relationships with animals now. Can't we in essence say it's the same as it was after the flood?

Yes, some animals have been domesticated, like dogs, who have developed to learn that *some* humans can be trusted. However, it takes time to tame wild animals and gain their trust. Think about the effort needed to get a robin to land on your hand and eat seed. We can't just tell them to obey us now. If we were to encounter a group of hippopotamuses in the wild, we wouldn't have the dominion, the authority, to rule over a hippo defending her calf and command her not to kill us. We would need to watch out!

This required a total change of perception for the women. No longer could they call a sheep towards them to shear its wool and it wouldn't wriggle and kick out to get away. They would need to guard their flocks against wolves, check their sandals for scorpions hiding inside. They would need to be protected from the hungry animals that wanted to eat them.

For more than a year on the ark they had looked after the animals, and now the majority of these would no longer be close to them. The flies Mert had been so protective about on the ark would now irritate her when they buzzed around the food. Sarah's birds would fly and hide in the trees. Just like Noah and his family, the animals had to adjust, adapt and make new homes for themselves on the earth.

Yet, though animals have a tendency to run away or hide, we're still fascinated by them. How many times do we find pleasure in observing the natural world? There is delight in seeing a colourful butterfly flutter around the garden, watching ants diligently work away, the sight of a red kite[53] soaring in the sky.

Comfort from nature was another theme of the pandemic. When and where we were able to, there relief was found through enjoying the beauty around us, from a countryside walk to spending more time in our gardens, or being able to notice the changes from the windows of our homes.

People often talk about being one with nature, and the reality is that before the flood, that's how we were. That's why we find such solace in it.

When we're able to bond with animals, it's special. I think we'd love to have that pre-flood relationship with the animals. It's almost an instinct we have if we see a wild animal to want to stroke it, but then we have to remember we can't. I'm glad to know that in the future God will restore the initial relationship we had with animals:

> The wolf and the lamb will graze together, and the lion will eat straw like the ox [there will no longer be predator and prey].
> (Isaiah 65:25)

That's something else to look forward to. In the meantime, while we manage animals for food or look after them as pets, Proverbs 12:10 tells us, 'A righteous man has kind regard for the life of his animal, But even the compassion of the wicked is

---

[53] A red kite is a bird of prey, hawkandowltrust.org/about-birds-of-prey/red-kite (accessed 28th October 2020).

cruel.' We see the evidence of this cruelty with how animals are treated across the world. The change God initiated after the flood doesn't give us a right to treat them unkindly – they are still His creation. He made space for them on the ark. His rainbow promise was also for them. Animals are important to God.

Another after-the-flood change

So Noah and his family had to get their heads around the changes with how animals were towards them, and that they could now eat them. Besides this, God established law. We don't know whether there was any form of government on the pre-flood earth. God certainly didn't give any authority for humanity to pass a judgement, such as when Cain killed Abel; instead He marked Cain so he wouldn't be harmed by anyone (Genesis 4:15).[54]

But in Genesis 9, God was putting in place accountability. He had already told Noah and his family in verse 4 they could now eat meat, but 'not eat meat along with its life, *that is*, its blood'. In the following verse, we see God would require an account from 'every animal [that kills a person]'. This is evidence that God knew animals would now kill people, but that He wouldn't forget those who do so.

I don't think God would have just said this for no reason. So however God does it, I expect that He does get that account from each animal who kills a person, whether this is a spider, shark or snake. I also think *more importantly*, that God is stressing to us that if He wants a shark to be accountable to Him for taking a person's life, then even more so a person who kills another person:

> And from man, from every man's brother [that is, anyone who murders] I will require the life of man.
> Whoever sheds man's blood [unlawfully],

---

54 Rice, *In the Beginning*, p 233.

By man (judicial government) shall his blood be shed,
For in the image of God
He made man.
(Genesis 9:5-6)

I'm not saying I take these Genesis verses as meaning someone should die because they've killed another person. But it does show the high value God places on human life, and also the care He's taking to establish sound principles. As it says here, this is about 'judicial government'. Remember, Noah's family had only just left the ark and God didn't want them killing each other. God had already witnessed what lawlessness looks like. He had destroyed 'every living thing' (Genesis 7:4), and now in those first few moments as humanity once again returned to the land, God sought to re-establish His principles for the post-flood earth they had stepped into.

Women are important to God

Think back to those unanswered questions Emzara might have had when Noah told her and their family about the flood, about how the women's plans were changed with the arrival of the unexpected, how even as they looked up at Mount Ararat and the ark resting in its peaks, they didn't know what their future looked like. The women could still only *work with what they knew*.

Whatever their role had been with the ark preparations, on the post-flood earth, their role was now even more important. They had new ground to manage; homes to establish; little ones to raise; meals to prepare with new meats, and all this among the dangers from wild animals.

God wanted women on the ark: we're important to Him.

When women get together, there can be a special bond. The joy we have chatting and laughing, catching up, crying together, supporting one another. There may be a tangible sense of sisterhood. Picture Emzara meeting up with her daughters-in-law, surrounded by her grandchildren; just like her ancestors, she loved to tell stories, passing down traditions. So nothing pleased her more than when one of the children ran over to her and said, 'Grandma, tell me about the rainbow again.'

The women of the ark story hadn't had the world's messages we hear about today, such as empowerment or breaking the glass ceiling, which may have their place, but we don't want to define ourselves or behave like the world says women should be. We want to be who we are: women of God.

Firstly, God made us, and when we read Genesis 2:21-22 we see how He took such care creating us; He fashioned and formed us. In Genesis 2:18 God speaks of the woman He would create as a 'helper [one who balances him – a counterpart who is] suitable *and* complementary for him'. The 'him' in this verse refers to Adam, but I don't think being referred to as a 'helper' means we're of any less worth than men. Consider where the verse says 'balances him'; in order for a woman to balance the man, a woman has to be the same weight. It's only when we have the same weight on both sides of a scale that they balance. I'm not talking about actual weight here! Women and men balance each other; that's the beauty of the differences between us and how we fit together.

I think Emzara and her daughters-in-law were strong and capable women, especially when we realise what they went through before, during and after the flood. On the post-flood earth, the women had to rise to constant new challenges and consider what was needed, as families moved away from the first homestead built after leaving the ark, as they explored the earth and resettled. We see throughout history what women have achieved, their hardships and victories.

When we study the Bible we read about nameless women and men in a mixture of roles. With every story, though, all the characters cannot be named, but this doesn't diminish who they are. Some of what we may perceive as the 'bigger' Bible stories are those of men, and I think what we hear in church, or the focus the world gives to Bible stories, may reinforce a false thought that men matter more. I'm sure Satan would love people to believe this lie because again it detracts from our Father's heart.

How we view what we do

Do we listen to the world saying we have to make a name for ourselves? Is it all about how we view what we do?

I've listened so many times to people concerned about what they do. The definition of themselves centres wholly on this; what they do defines them: striving to make an impression, to be noticed, validated and appreciated. I've felt that way too.

How much does it feel like our work lives and progress are measured on the amount of doing? I'm not saying hard work isn't right, but there is such a strong, worldly push to do, do and do even more. But there is only so much we can do, and if we can't stop ourselves, there is a real risk of burning out, which totally eradicates everything we're striving for.

I've had jobs where it's felt like the role didn't fit me and I was unsettled. When we feel this way it rocks us, especially if we don't actually know what other job we'd like instead, but we still have to get up and go to work to earn money, even though we know something isn't quite right.

This feeling doesn't have to be just work; it can be in any of our circumstances when we feel like we should be doing something else, we don't feel satisfied, or we feel like we're missing out on who we really are. That feeling of unsettlement in our circumstances may not always be wrong. Sometimes it can be a nudge to get us thinking about another direction. But when the feeling overtakes us and upsets us, makes us feel low and hopeless, trapped, then that can't be right. What if we can't make an immediate change?

What mirror are we holding up to ourselves? Is our view skewed? It's all about altering the angle of *how we view what we do*, and these are some of the things that can help us when we feel this way.

Remind ourselves of the difference between happiness and joy

We may not be happy emotionally where we are, but happiness is a feeling that can be temporary. If our situation doesn't make us happy, then we need to think about what we really mean by that. What is it that's actually going on to create that emotion? That's more important to understand than making impetuous decisions based on our 'happy meter'. We need to make decisions based on His peace:

> Let the peace of Christ [the inner calm of one who walks daily with Him] be the controlling factor in your hearts [deciding and settling questions that arise].
> (Colossians 3:15)

It's His peace that helps us to remain calm and settled, even when we don't feel anything like this – even when we wake up and think, 'What am I doing?' And remember, we may not always be happy in every moment of our day, but it doesn't mean we can't be joyful. We spoke in Chapter Six about 'the joy of the LORD' being our strength (Nehemiah 8:10), and that doesn't go away in these situations; that's what we need to hold on to, the joy we have in Him.

Adjust the zoom

We need to pull back the focus from the dissatisfaction we feel about what we do. Minimise it. There are many parts to us, but when we feel like this, we can tend to lump everything together. When we change the angle, we'll be able to step back and have time to consider other things. This might help to reveal something that was not within our immediate vision.

Keep going with it

Ecclesiastes 9:10 says, 'Whatever your hand finds to do, do *it* with all your might' (italics mine). Many times we can't make immediate changes in this kind of situation. It takes time.

Actually the time, though frustrating, can be helpful because once we're aware our view is skewed, then we can work through the situation with the Lord. While we're doing this, we keep going with our 'it', and the liberating key is to do *it* for Him (Colossians 3:23). Whatever *it* we're facing today, doing *it* for the Lord breaks the power over how *it* makes us feel. We're not stuck. What we're doing doesn't make up all of who we are. We're important to God. He will give us wisdom to help us move on.

Who women are

There are many skills and abilities that make us the individually talented women we are. Though Genesis may not tell us about who the women of the ark story were, Proverbs 31:10-31 gives us more description. Though the verses are written in the setting of the woman being a wife, I think it tells us about who women are and the attributes we have.

I've reflected on the verses and thought about how we'd translate what the Bible says into the language we'd use today to describe what she does. So we might say she was:

- an entrepreneur;

- financially astute;

- a project manager;

- an experienced organiser;

- a leader and teacher;

- strategic and forward-thinking;

- a negotiator;

- good with people and at communicating;

- able to see the bigger picture;

- reflective on events;

- adaptive to change;

- willing to learn;

- a role model and mentor to others;

- a carer; and

- kind, encouraging, generous and brave.

Help, I'm beginning to compare myself to the list, but that's not a good idea! So instead, let's explore some more about what she actually does.

Proverbs 31:16 says, 'She considers a field before she buys or accepts it [expanding her business prudently].' Yes, it makes us think about the literal act of handling money. I can remember the times I've rushed to buy something and then regretted it. However, here in Proverbs 31 the woman uses her money wisely through assessing the circumstances. She takes the time to discern and evaluate, and she's doing this in relation to business – she's a businesswoman.

Even back in the Old Testament, look at the many skills being displayed by women! We can see this when we observe history. Women have often been pioneers, at the forefront of discoveries, or have managed vast estates. Think of Katherine Johnson and Dr Christine Darden at NASA whose mathematical and technological skills enabled astronauts to go into space in the middle of the twentieth century.[55] Then in the sixteenth century there was Bess of Hardwick who had a zeal for designing and building properties in Derbyshire.[56]

It doesn't mean we all have to be like this, or feel bad if we're not; we're all uniquely different, but in our multifaceted abilities,

---

[55] Dr Dava Newman and Dr Ellen Stofan, 'Women Have Always Been NASA Pioneers', NASA, 17th March 2016,
blogs.nasa.gov/leadership/2016/03/17/women-have-always-been-nasa-pioneers/ (accessed 28th October 2020).
[56] 'Bess of Hardwick', English Heritage, www.english-heritage.org.uk/learn/histories/women-in-history/bess-of-hardwick/ (accessed 28th October 2020).

women have an aptitude for many things. And returning to the Proverbs woman, is she doing all these things in her own strength?

Proverbs 31:10 tell us she is 'An excellent woman [one who is spiritual, capable, intelligent, and virtuous]'. Notice 'spiritual' is emphasised first before any other characteristics. Later on in the verses:

> She equips herself with strength [spiritual, mental, and
> physical fitness for her God-given task]
> And makes her arms strong.
> (Proverbs 31:17)

Irrespective of everything else on the list, the first type of strength she needs is 'spiritual'. Perhaps it is strengthening her spirit that actually enables her to build her mind and body so those arms become muscular and powerful?

We also get an insight into how she views her work – it's her assignment from the Lord. This isn't a woman doing all of this for doing's sake. She's prepared for the 'God-given' project at hand, whether this is making business decisions, raising her children or understanding how to support/balance out her husband. Remember, though, the variety of activities she's doing: working wool, managing the household, buying a field and planting vines (Proverbs 31:13, 15, 16).

We need to equip ourselves, too. We need to make our arms strong. We need to wisely seek spiritual strength first and then whatever else is needed for the responsibilities in our lives. These verses in Proverbs 31 aren't about a woman who has been blessed with all of these attributes, but a woman who primarily has a relationship with God and is eager to learn and develop herself.

Let this be the encouragement we can take. We may not all be able to be wives or mothers, but we are women; let our lives demonstrate that we are women who fear the Lord: '[reverently worshiping, obeying, serving, and trusting Him with awe-filled respect], she shall be praised' (Proverbs 31:30).

Unlike the woman whose 'lamp does not go out, but it burns continually through the night [she is prepared for whatever lies ahead]' (Proverbs 31:18), when they stepped off the ark, Emzara, Tia, Sarah and Mert would have not been prepared for all the changes that faced them. As they settled into the days, weeks and months of after-the-flood life, into that new unknown, the unfamiliarity of the first pregnancy, motherhood, all Noah and his family could do was trust. But we can see the evidence of their fruitfulness around us. We are testament to it. At present there are 7.8 billion people in the world.[57] All the descendants of those three women. Incredible.

This isn't just because Tia, Sarah and Mert were mothers; it is because they were women. Because of their unique abilities and talents. The skills passed down, as generation turned into generations.

There are many achievements of women in history, but over and above those who are known and we can learn about are the many unspoken nameless women of faith who've lived each day, trusting the Lord to equip them for each challenge. Let's not torture ourselves with analysing our lives through *what we do*, but instead place ourselves into our Father's care:

> How blessed *and* greatly favored is the *[woman]* who trusts in You [believing in You, relying on You, and committing *[herself]* to You with confident hope and expectation].
> (Psalm 84:12)[58]

[57] 'Current World Population', Worldometer, www.worldometers.info/world-population/ (accessed 28th October 2020).
[58] Author's additions in italicised square brackets.

Father, thank You so much for all the understanding we can gain from this Genesis chapter. Thank You for making me a woman, and as a woman, You've made me with so many beautiful layers of complexities and colours. Help me when I feel unsettled, help me to change my view about what I do, bring me back to You being at the centre of everything, and remind me of the joy You alone give. Help me to appreciate myself and the skills I alone have. I trust that You will continue to guide me in how I use and grow them. I ask all this knowing that the passionate prayers of a faith-filled woman are effective.[59]

Amen.

---

[59] Author's paraphrase of James 5:16, NKJV.

Chapter contemplations

- Arrange to gather with friends and/or family to delight in the pleasure of eating together, knowing God delights in food too.

- Think about the changes God initiated for the post-flood earth. There's a lot to digest from Genesis 9, so take some time to reflect.

- Read Proverbs 31:10-31. What skills can you identify with? Are there any others that could be added to the list? Have some journal time noting your thoughts. Also, ask Jesus about how you can either learn new skills or develop those you already have.

Journal pages

11
Are There Always Giants?

We could leave the story of the flood after the rainbow appeared in the sky. We could imagine Noah's descendants dispersing throughout the world. We could assume everything after the flood on the earth was perfect – but we know everything wasn't.

Noah's vineyard

Near the end of Genesis 9 we're told, 'Noah began to farm *and* cultivate the ground and he planted a vineyard' (Genesis 9:20). It's an activity you'd imagine as they established themselves on the earth; they didn't wait to settle back into their lives. So why does the Bible tell us this?

It shows us the family continued to use the skills they had before they entered the ark. They still needed to work the ground to grow food and crops for the animals they'd kept, not only for offerings and clothing now, but also to eat. Among all the hubbub, grandchildren running around and ground being cultivated, there was Noah thinking about wine.

We've already considered how much change was introduced in Genesis 9 when the family left the ark, and it also shows us that we don't have to read that much further before we start to see there were problems. This passage isn't necessarily about Noah's vineyard, but more about what happened afterwards.

Noah's wine

There are different views about when wine-making first started in the world, yet here in these early after-the-flood days, Noah 'planted a vineyard'. This makes me think it's highly likely that Noah grew grapes before the flood if he wanted to grow them now. Perhaps wine-making knowledge had been passed down through his forebears. There are references to wine throughout the Bible: from the offerings made by the priests (Exodus 29:40) to 'wine which makes the heart of man glad' (Psalm 104:15) and wisdom about not overconsuming it (Isaiah 5:11).

Though we're told in Genesis 9:20 that 'Noah planted a vineyard', we can presume because the next verse goes straight into when Noah drank some wine that little time had passed. Though the earth was fruitful, it takes time to establish vines. Wine doesn't just happen from harvesting grapes and drinking their juice. They need to be fermented to develop the alcohol. A period of three years can pass from when vines are first planted to harvesting the fruit and then another two years before it can be stored.[60] So however Noah made his wine, there still would have been a wine-making process to be followed.

Genesis also gives us an indication of time passing by the mention of Ham's son, Canaan (Genesis 9:22), and we know from Genesis 10:6 that Ham had three sons before he had Canaan. So I believe there was a period of years while the vines grew, grapes were harvested and the juice fermented. Whatever age vintage of wine Noah chose to drink, he 'drank some of the wine and became drunk, and he was uncovered *and* lay exposed inside his tent' (Genesis 9:21).

This is the first clue we have that post-flood life wouldn't be perfect. This is the first time the Bible tells us about a weakness in Noah. Not necessarily in him drinking the wine he'd made, but drinking enough to get intoxicated. There is a possibility that

---

[60] Alexa K Apallas, 'The Life Cycle of a Wine Grape: From Planting to Harvest to Bottle', Winecooler Direct, 6th July 2016, learn.winecoolerdirect.com/life-cycle-of-a-wine-grape/ (accessed 2nd November 2020).

Noah hadn't drunk such alcoholic wine before, even though he knew about tending a vineyard. This could have been the first time he'd let the juice ferment. Irrespective of whether this was Noah's first sip of wine or he ended up drinking a vat of his vintage, he still got drunk on this occasion, and a bit more than drunk too. Here was a man who habitually walked with God, who was the only one whom God found blameless when He cast His eyes upon the pre-flood earth. And now here he was, passed out in a stupor. It's an image that doesn't exactly equate, does it? But it's so reassuring. Really?

Yes, you see, Noah wasn't God. Noah was a man. A human, just like us, with all of our strengths and weaknesses. Noah wasn't perfect. Neither was his family.

Ham's temptation

Noah must have been alone in the tent when he fell asleep and remained lying there uncovered. Though he probably did learn a lesson about the danger of wine and what kind of behaviour it can cause,[61] I don't think this is what the example is all about because something else happened.

His youngest son Ham passed by with Japheth and Shem. Ham didn't expect to see his father in that situation, but perhaps he peered inside the tent, wondering where Noah was, and 'by accident' saw 'the nakedness of his father' (Genesis 9:22). Big deal?

I mean, if that was me, my eyes would quickly snap shut and I'd hurry on, wanting to pretend I hadn't just seen what I had. If Ham had done that, it wouldn't have been a problem. But, no, he didn't. He made the choice to tell Japheth and Shem. Maybe he laughed and said, 'Guess who's in here, brothers! Abba is passed out, snoring and naked.'

We could say the choice Ham made was like confronting a giant. Not a giant who'd kill him, but a giant who tempted Ham to do something he knew he shouldn't do. Ham was a father

---

[61] Rice, *In the Beginning*, p 239.

too. Would he have wanted his own children to embarrass him like that? Something in Ham couldn't stop himself from shaming Noah and showing no regard for his parent.[62] And giving in to that giant meant it wasn't Ham who paid the price. No, it was Ham's son, Canaan.

What about Ham's brothers, Japheth and Shem? Consider their reaction to what Ham told them. They didn't laugh along with Ham. They didn't quickly look inside the tent to check he had told them the truth. They made the choice to use a robe and placed it around 'both their shoulders' like a cloak, and reversed into the tent, deliberately keeping their eyes averted so they caught no accidental sight of their father's naked body when they covered him (Genesis 9:23).

We've explored the characteristics of women, the many dimensions of our skills and character. This verse reveals the inner man of Japheth and Shem. Their sense of honour, their desire for Noah not to be embarrassed and their brotherly relationship. It was the two of them who together covered their father – they supported each other. They didn't cast lots to see who would go inside the tent.

How did Noah know it was Ham?

Noah eventually woke up covered with a robe he knew wasn't his. Did Noah get up thinking, 'Who has done this? Did Emzara cover me? I hope one of the little ones didn't see me.' No, Noah 'knew what his younger son [Ham] had done to him' (Genesis 9:24). How did Noah know it was Ham?

Noah knew what his son was like. He must have known enough about Ham's behaviour to think it was him. Why? Because Noah didn't have to struggle to come up with a culprit, it wasn't a surprise for him to immediately think, 'Ham has seen me and told his brothers.' This doesn't place Ham's character in a good light. It suggests this kind of conduct from Ham wasn't

---

[62] Ibid, pp 239-240.

new, and maybe this was the final act for Noah, provoking him enough to want to curse his grandchild.

The consequence of Ham's choice

Ham's action resulted in his father saying:

> 'Cursed be Canaan [the son of Ham];
> A servant of servants
> He shall be to his brothers.'
> He also said,
> 'Blessed be the LORD,
> The God of Shem;
> And let Canaan be his servant.
> May God enlarge [the land of] Japheth,
> And let him dwell in the tents of Shem;
> And let Canaan be his servant.'
> (Genesis 9:25-27)

It is interesting that Noah chose to curse his grandson Canaan but blessed his children, Shem and Japheth. Notice the wording, though. Noah was being prophetic here in the words he spoke. Noah blessed the Lord and declared Him the God of Shem. He didn't know at that point that Jesus or the Jewish people would be descended from Shem's line. When we're given Jesus's genealogy in Luke 3:23-38, there are some familiar names in the passage: Jesus is the 'son of *Shem*, the son of *Noah*', with more generations leading to 'the son of Seth, the son of Adam, the son of God' (Luke 3:36, 38, italics mine). Then Japheth is blessed – if God is the God of Shem, then by Japheth dwelling in Shem's tents, God will be his God too.

And what Noah prophesied happened, but not immediately. Canaan got married, had children, his generational line continued. Indeed, there are many mentions of the land of Canaan or the Canaanites in the Bible. Joshua tells us they were a strong people and had iron chariots (Joshua 17:18). Psalms speaks of the Canaanites being a pagan people (Psalm 106:34).

God had to destroy Sodom and Gomorrah, which were morally corrupt cities in the land of Canaan (Genesis 10:19).

We spoke before about the promise given to Abraham that his descendants would 'inherit the land of Canaan'.[63] He was Shem's descendant (Genesis 11:10-31), born ten generations after Noah,[64] and was the recipient of the earlier blessing given to his forefather.

There is so much depth here, isn't there? What Noah said didn't result in an immediate consequence, but instead a foretelling of what would take place and which is manifested later on in the Bible. All because of Ham's choice not to ignore what he had seen and instead to make a mockery of it to his brothers.

I wonder what happened after Noah cursed Canaan and blessed Japheth and Shem. Did Noah tell his sons what he'd said? The Bible doesn't say they were there when Noah woke, so they may not have been immediately aware of the blessings and curse. Whether or not they knew, I think what happened with Ham's behaviour would have been a trigger, even subconsciously, to eventually prompt the brothers to move away, particularly Ham. Even if Noah's words may have sparked that desire, I think the consequences of them lit a fire of jealousy between his kin.

So why did God save Noah?

You could say that it was Noah's fault in this example because he was the one who got drunk in the first place. I'm sure Ham must have wanted to pass the blame on to someone else too. What we learn from this is that it didn't take Noah and his family long after leaving the ark to demonstrate the behaviour that had been there on the pre-flood earth. We see humanity's fallibility.

---

[63] Taken from *Halley's Bible Handbook* by Dr Henry H Halley Copyright © 1965 by Dr Henry H Halley. Used by permission of Zondervan, www.zondervan.com, p 94.

[64] Rice, *In the Beginning*, p 253.

After the flood, sin hadn't left the earth; they were still living in a fallen world. The flood was a judgement because the overwhelming majority of people had turned away from wanting to know or even acknowledge God. Yet it didn't remove humankind's fleshly propensity for sin. God knew when He spoke to Noah and told him to build an ark that many, many years later Noah would get drunk. That Ham's moral character would mean he'd shame his father. Still God chose to save Noah and his family. And if God hadn't saved Noah, then we wouldn't be here and many, many generations later we wouldn't have our Saviour, Jesus.

God wanted us, even though He knew we would mess up and make mistakes. And because of His love for us, He gave us the only way out of sin: 'For this is how God loved the world: He gave his one and only Son' (John 3:16, NLT). Jesus conquered the power of sin over our lives. He took the burden sin places on us when He died and rose again from the dead. At the cross, all sin was forgiven: past, present and future. Jesus said, 'It is finished' (John 19:30) and 'everyone who believes in him will have their sins forgiven through his name' (Acts 10:43, NLT).

This doesn't mean as believers we'll never sin again. We are still living in our fleshly bodies, but it does mean we can go to Him for forgiveness. It's Jesus' power that loosens us from the shame and control sin has in our lives: 'So if the Son sets you free, you are truly free' (John 8:36, NLT).

Giants after the flood

When Ham shamed his father, it was like a giant tempting him, but were there actual giants on the post-flood earth?

Let's think about before the flood first. Genesis 6:4 implies there were giants then because it mentions:

> Nephilim (men of stature, notorious men) on the earth in those days – and also afterward – when the sons of

God lived with the daughters of men, and they gave
birth to their *children*.

'Nephilim' could refer to giants in this verse because of the word 'stature', but there are various opinions about who the 'sons of God' were, such as whether they were fallen angels or other children of Seth.[65] Setting aside this question about where the Nephilim came from, which I can't answer here, I think it's likely there were giants before the flood, but they would have been killed in it.

We know that only eight people survived on the ark, so if there were any actual giants after the flood, these would have come from Noah's descendants. And when we read the Old Testament we can find accounts of people who were considerably tall and of a strong build. What I find interesting is that some of these giants were from Ham's lineage. The Zuzim resided in the land of Ham (Genesis 14:5), and were a group of tall people; in Deuteronomy 2:20-21 it refers to the Zanzummim being as 'great, numerous … and tall as the Anakim'. [66] Another one of Ham's grandsons, Nimrod, is described as being 'a mighty one on the earth' (Genesis 10:8), and 'mighty' implies strength through size. It makes me wonder if Ham passed on height as a physical trait to some of his children.

In certain Bible translations, the word 'Nephilim' is used again to refer to giants after the flood (Numbers 13:33). This can cause confusion when we think about the 'sons of God' context and there isn't a consensus about what the Hebrew

---

65 Bodie Hodge, 'Nephilim: Who Were They?' Answers in Genesis, 9th July 2008, answersingenesis.org/bible-characters/who-were-the-nephilim/ (accessed 2nd November 2020). Permission given from Answers in Genesis.
66 Tim Chaffey, 'Giants in the Bible', Answers in Genesis, 22nd February 2012, answersingenesis.org/bible-characters/giants-in-the-bible/ (accessed 14th October 2020). Permission given from Answers in Genesis. Note, the article's author says the names Zuzim and Zamzummin can be used interchangeably.

word means.[67] I think 'Nephilim' is used in this verse as a comparison for people who had a giant-like appearance rather than a literal interpretation.

Regardless as to who the Nephilim were, there is biblical evidence about humans who had the appearance and size of giants on the post-flood earth. Though it's rarer for us to see someone we would think of as a giant in the world today, it doesn't mean we won't have giants in our lives.

Emotional giants in our lives

Though we're not going to come across the Zuzim, we will come across other giants. So, what giants do I mean?

I'm not referring to people who are tall, but to emotions that are like giants to us. Their significance and stature makes us feel scared and small. These kinds of giants come in all shapes and sizes. Sometimes we know them. Sometimes they appear when we're unaware. What may feel like a giant to one person doesn't to another. It's how we perceive them.

When I think of an emotional giant, I get a reaction: fear. It's a natural instinct to feel afraid of something, especially if it's a lot larger than us, or appears that way.

The question about what to do next feels like a giant to me. It appears like the tempting kind of giant that Ham faced in the tent. It taunts and jeers, wanting to lure me away, to give in... ultimately it's wanting me to react. Isn't that what giving in to temptation is? You're tempted by the box of chocolates so you 'give in' and eat some.

When this giant looms, it's always when I'm feeling vulnerable about my state of uncertainty, or I've been triggered to compare myself to someone else who seems to have a plan; other times, the giant comes uninvited. I get a fearful and panicked reaction because I think I'm being inactive. I want to jump, pounce on something, anything, to make me feel like I'm

---

[67] Bodie Hodge, 'Nephilim: Who Were They?' Answers in Genesis, 9th July 2008. Permission given from Answers in Genesis.

making progress. I look beyond the what-I'm-doing-today into the great unknown of tomorrow.

These kinds of emotional giants are common around the times when we have doubts or feel insecure. It may not always be about what we do next in our lives, such as work, but those kinds of situations when we don't know, and when we think about them too much, we're frightened.

When we're afraid, the fear we feel can make our bodies respond and we experience a physical reaction.[68] The hormones pumping round our bodies are there to help us run away from a threatening situation, so it's not surprising that we want to do something when we feel the fear. I have learned to remind myself each time not to react immediately, not to think I need to suddenly start searching for jobs, worry about whether I'm networking enough or even worry that I'm not quite sure what to do.

Unless I acknowledge the emotion, though, it's very easy to get diverted into the reaction and to find myself doing things for the wrong reason. What we have to remember is that Jesus is in control when we feel this way, even if we have to say it aloud or whisper it to ourselves: 'Jesus, You're in control. I am moving forward, even if I can't feel any motion.' Usually, I find reminding myself like this halts the giant in its tracks, and stops me from wanting to act, or pursuing the action I've started. Why?

Because when we say to the giant, 'God's in control,' we're not letting ourselves be overtaken by the fear it brings: 'For God has not given us a spirit of fear, but of power and of love and of a sound mind' (2 Timothy 1:7, NKJV). That's what we do when we remind ourselves that in Him we have a 'sound mind'. We don't need to be provoked by fearful reactions.

When Jesus was with His disciples, they frequently referred to Him as a teacher (Mark 4:38). Jesus is many things, but He

---

[68] 'Fight-or-Flight Response', Britannica, www.britannica.com/science/fight-or-flight-response (accessed 2nd November 2020).

also said, 'You call Me Teacher and Lord, and you are right in doing so, for *that is who* I am' (John 13:13). The reality is that, in our walk with Jesus, we're in a state of learning, and what I love is that Jesus is more than happy to teach me. So if we're constantly in that frame of mind, eager to learn, to develop, to grow with Him, then it allows Him to teach us, because His 'strength is made perfect in [our] weakness' (2 Corinthians 12:9, NKJV, addition mine).

The giants we want to fight

We all know one post-flood giant. Remember him?

Yes, you've got it: Goliath.

It's a Bible story, which is familiar, but for me what stands out is how young David approached his fight with Goliath. David had confidence in approaching him with just his sling and five stones. And in spite of the bronze helmet Goliath wore, it was the first stone sent from David's sling that hit Goliath's forehead and killed him (1 Samuel 17:5, 49).

Goliath thought he was safe against anything and anyone, not only because his size made him so physically intimidating, but also because of how much protection he wore. When Goliath saw David he ridiculed him and thought David had no worth as an opponent (1 Samuel 17:42). Yet with the first sling shot, David's small stone found its target.

With emotional giants we don't see them, but there are events in our lives that are like giants to us through the challenges they present. They make us feel like we have to fight against them. We arm ourselves with swords and spears and prepare ourselves for the battle.

Do we actually need to fight our giants, though?

David chose to use the sling which he had used many times before to keep bears from attacking his flocks of sheep. The words he stated to Saul about God rescuing him, and then declared when he went out to meet Goliath, reveal who David relied on: 'for the battle is the LORD's' (1 Samuel 17:37, 47). Though David went to fight Goliath, he declared that it was actually the Lord's battle. In essence, though David's sling cast the stone, it was 'the Lord' who won the battle.

Therefore, we can't defeat giants ourselves, and neither should we try to strategise how we should fight them: 'Not by might, nor by power, but by My Spirit' (Zechariah 4:6). It's the Lord and the Holy Spirit in us who'll help us know the approach. We may want to load ourselves up with weapons, or people will give us heavy protection to wear, as Saul tried with David (1 Samuel 17:38-39). But is a simple stone all we need?

The small stone that will always help us win when we see that giant in front of us is listening to the sound of His 'still small voice' (1 Kings 19:12, NKJV).

Are all giants bad?

Have you ever played the whack-a-mole game? You know, the game where moles (not real ones!) keep popping out of holes and you have to whack them with a hammer. As soon as you've hit one, then another mole appears, and another and another...

Well, our trip to America felt like that. Once we'd prayerfully made the decision to go, suddenly there were all sorts of problems and challenges in front of us. I don't think it's a coincidence when this happens.

My mum said to me one time about how she felt there were all these giants and they kept appearing. Some of them now appear simple with hindsight, but they sure didn't at the time. With each issue that arose we had to trust the Lord and not let them intimidate us. Some giants were from the enemy. Some were emotional. Some were real. We were concerned about Mum's health with the long flight on the plane; whether she could get travel insurance; choosing dates; who to fly with; logistics of arranging everything; how we'd get to the airport... wham... wham... wham... we whacked those giants... then more appeared.

It wasn't easy, and at times it was overwhelming with everything and then thinking, 'But what if that happened?' Sometimes we were able to whack the emotional giant, but mostly it was a case of reassuring ourselves about the goodness of the Lord, and that He was bringing to reality that *sense of soon* I had felt a few years before.

After the months of planning, we got to the airport, having first stayed with my mum's family who lived nearby – no stress of having to think about how to get there for the early flight! We got through security with all the medicine, boarded the plane at Heathrow, the trip becoming more of a reality with each stage we passed. We hadn't been guaranteed bulkhead seats, though we'd requested them, but when we checked in we found out they had been assigned to us, so Mum had the leg space she needed. On the flight, the cabin crew were considerate of her needs, and we eventually landed in Washington DC. The person was waiting with the wheelchair when we left the plane – another worry giant (would they be there?). As we moved away I spotted the name of the plane we'd just travelled in, and part of the name included the word 'love'. I don't know what the people thought around me but I laughed aloud because 'love' stood out strongly to me. I can remember the Holy Spirit confirming in my spirit how the plane's name summed up the Lord's love for the trip and His purpose behind it. He'd even flown us across the Atlantic on a plane called love! God was so kind, caring for us through all the fears, worries, problems and concerns those giants gave. I'm sure He was busy whacking away other unseen giants too.

You know what, I'm so thankful for all those giants. How can I be? Because it was another moment of growth in my relationship with Him. The situation taught me how much I needed to rely on the Lord for His strength as I pushed through, ignored and ran towards the giants armed with the strategy He gave me. It didn't mean I wasn't afraid, didn't get upset or that the problems weren't real, but with His grace, I was able to face the giants.

Facing our giants

Another big lesson I'm learning, and it is an ongoing process, is how I face the giants that present in my life. When I think of some of the worries I had with the America trip, and how the Lord overcame them, I wonder what would have happened if I'd allowed myself to worry less and trust in His promises more. We know that Jesus has already defeated the giants in our lives.

What do I mean?

At the cross, Jesus obtained total victory for us in every area of our lives. Whatever the size of giant in our lives, He is greater (1 John 4:4). He is 'higher than anything and anyone' (Psalm 113:4, *The Message*).

But we may not always feel or see that manifestation immediately, and when we don't, we may want to react, solve, defeat or control the giant we face. I'm also conscious that saying, 'Face your giants,' sounds like the world's way of saying, 'Face your fears'; that somehow putting our hands into a jar full of spiders or standing on a tall building's glass roof will cure us. But that's relying on the strength of our flesh, and we know our flesh is weak, however much we think we can humanly overcome:

> For those who live according to the flesh set their minds
> on the things of the flesh, but those *who live* according
> to the Spirit, the things of the Spirit.
> (Romans 8:5, NKJV)

If we set our minds on how our flesh can handle the giants, then we can get ourselves in all kinds of mess. Because we're relying on how we think we should face them. When I think about facing giants, I'm reminded of Moses and the Israelite people in the desert. Before they had left Egypt, God had said to Moses about bringing the Israelites into:

> the land of the Canaanite, the Hittite, the Amorite, the
> Hivite, and the Jebusite, which He swore to your fathers

to give you, a land [of abundance] flowing with milk and honey.
(Exodus 13:5)

This is the Promised Land for the Jewish people. God is reminding Moses in this verse about the land that He had given to Abraham and Isaac, and then to Jacob (Genesis 35:12). We can trace God's promise about Israel right back to the day when Ham told his brothers about Noah and the subsequent blessing Noah proclaimed on to Shem's line. We know Abraham was a descendant of Shem,[69] and so was Isaac, Abraham's son, and Jacob, his grandson (Genesis 11:10; 21:3; 25:26).

In Numbers 13:2, after Moses and the Israelites have left Egypt, God says to Moses, 'Send men to spy out the land of Canaan, which I am going to give to the sons of Israel.' This wasn't a new message about Canaan. Moses must have been aware when God told him that they were so close to the land that God had promised. Moses sent twelve spies out. For forty days the spies traversed the land, taking note of everything they saw, and they cut off a branch filled with large, ripe grapes and brought this back along with pomegranates and figs (Numbers 13:23-24).

Moses, Aaron and the rest of the Israelites waited for them to return. When they did, the spies reported back, 'We went in to the land where you sent us; and it certainly does flow with milk and honey, and this is its fruit' (Numbers 13:27). The spies repeated exactly how God had described the land earlier to Moses as 'flowing with milk and honey' (Exodus 13:5). Surely this land had to be it? The spies continued with their account. But there was a 'but':

> *But the people living there are powerful,* and their towns are large and fortified. We even saw giants there, the descendants of Anak!
> (Numbers 13:28, NLT, italics mine)

---

[69] Shem was Abraham's great-great-great-great-great-great-great-grandfather.

What does this 'But' create? The crowd grew noisy, shouting questions, exclaiming to each other, shaking their heads. There was no time for them to digest the wonderful news of a land abundant 'with milk and honey'. Why? Because of the giants. They were so big, the spies said they felt like grasshoppers compared to them (Numbers 13:33). Suddenly there was fear, worry and confusion.

Caleb tried to hush the crowd. "'Let's go at once to take the land," he said. "We can certainly conquer it!'" (Numbers 13:30, NLT). Caleb trusted. But no, still the other spies focused on the giants when telling the story about the land. The spies emphasised again to the crowd about the land devouring its inhabitants and the men being of 'great stature' (Numbers 13:32). The Israelites got themselves worked up and spent the night weeping and wondering why they were to be killed by these mighty men. They even wanted to return to Egypt (Numbers 14:1-4).

The next day Joshua tried again to speak to the crowd like Caleb had the day before. He reminded the Israelites about the land. He said they didn't need to fear the giants. The people didn't listen, though; instead they wanted to stone Joshua and Caleb (Numbers 14:10).

It seems to me that the people had truly set their minds on 'things of the flesh' here (Romans 8:5). We can see this in the Israelites' reaction to what the spies said, what they subsequently thought overnight, and then being so fleshly enraged with Joshua and Caleb that all they wanted to do was kill them, even though all they were doing was believing in what God had said – that they could face these giants.

The Israelites' reaction to the size of the giants meant they never went into the Promised Land; instead, God told them they would die in the wilderness, with another forty years of wandering around the desert (Numbers 14:30-32). Of course, once the people knew this, they didn't like the sound of that. So what did some of them do? They tried to go and fight the giants in their own might, in their strength. But the Lord wasn't with them in this battle of their own endeavours and those who went back into the land were killed by its inhabitants (Numbers 14:40-45).

Eventually, though, the forty years passed and we can read in the books of Deuteronomy and Joshua about those years and how Joshua, Caleb and all of the Israelites' children[70] entered into the Canaanites' land.

None of this period in the desert would have happened if they'd trusted in God's promise to them rather than relying on their initial instinct.

Facing our giants with trust

Trust.

It's easy to say 'trust' when often, humanly speaking, it takes a lot for us to fully trust people.

There is a 'trust fall' exercise you might have heard about or seen, where people fall backwards with someone standing behind to catch them in their arms. It's meant to build up the feeling of trust in a team or people you're working with, but I certainly wouldn't attempt it unless I was certain the person standing behind would and could catch me. I'd need to know I could trust them.

There are so many connotations when we think of giving our trust to people. And often when we trust them, we can find the trust is broken. As the pattern repeats over time, we learn to build a wall around trust and the amount we give: we want to protect ourselves. We've fallen backwards too many times and not been caught. So how do we *trust that God* is reliable, truthful and able? Can we ask ourselves to trust Him when we may find it hard to trust others?

An extract from my journal before the America trip reads:

---

[70] God said the Israelites' children would enter who were aged nineteen or under (Numbers 14:29). See Numbers 20:11-12 for why Moses and Aaron didn't lead the Israelites into the land.

It's coming back to trust – a total lack of my control. Like saying I trust in the Lord our hold luggage won't get lost, but then taking medicine back-ups anyway. It's going beyond the glib meaning, the flippant statement, right down to the core of do I really mean this?

How can we really mean it when we say we trust the Lord?

Because trusting the Lord is different from how we trust people – we say it in faith. When we're trusting in the Lord, as we face our giants we need to remember:

We don't want to talk ourselves out of trust

We can give more airtime to our giants by thinking and talking about all the things that confront us, rather than talking about what is good (Philippians 4:8). Talking about our giant isn't going to make God work any faster or inform Him more. He already knows. Though it's good to share our problems with others, we need to remember the power of words. If all we're doing is speaking negatively, choosing words that aren't full of life, the giant is going to appear insurmountable. Don't let's talk ourselves out of trust or make the giants appear even bigger than they are.

The blessing of trust

Satan will want us to doubt ourselves. He'll question us, 'You'd better do something just to be sure.' The enemy makes us feel like we need to retain that grip on whatever we're trusting God about, but when we trust God it brings along a blessing, a secure foundation, which enables us to have confidence in Him (Jeremiah 17:7). This is what we need to base our certainty on, rather than the unsteadiness of our emotional state.

We don't want to rely on our instincts

The Israelites' instinct when they reacted to the spies' account of the Promised Land was to say, 'We can't defeat those mighty giants.' They were self-reliant, perhaps even proud. They didn't want to risk going into the land and not winning the battle. Sometimes it's easier to trust ourselves more, to be confident in our own assessment of the situation, and to retain our self-control. It comes back to when we've been hurt and we want to protect ourselves. We can only trust what we think is best. It takes an act of self-will to humble ourselves, to say, 'I will trust in Jesus' – but we can, because we're women of faith; we believe in Him.

You see, when we supercharge trust with hope, max it out further with faith and then give it a final boost with knowing we're secure in His unconditional love, then it becomes part of who we are. In our relationship with Him we can wholeheartedly say, 'But as for me, I trust [confidently] in You *and* Your greatness, O LORD; I *[say]*,[71] "You are my God"' (Psalm 31:14).

Looking back

What can also strengthen our trust in the Lord is looking back at our lives.

If the Israelites had remembered all of the miracles they'd experienced in Egypt and after they'd left, surely this would have increased their hope? That God who'd parted the Red Sea for them to safely cross over would enable them to go up against any sized giant (Exodus 14:21)?

I wonder whether in those days, after Ham had shamed his father, Noah had to remind himself about all that had happened with building the ark and the flood, to remember all God had done, in dealing with any emotional after-effects from Ham's behaviour.

Have you ever visited somewhere new and you've been so eager to explore all your surroundings and see the sights that you don't realise how much you've walked or driven? It's only when you look at a map, or check your phone, that you realise how far you've gone.

---

[71] Author's addition in italicised square brackets.

217

Our lives can be so busy, stressful and demanding that we don't have time to reflect. And it's only when we look back that we realise how many steps we've taken or what was happening when we actually took them. Reflecting prompts us to look at the Lord, to praise Him, to be thankful for what He has already done in our lives, and *to remind us He can do those deeds again*. As David says:

> But then I recall all you have done, O LORD;
> I remember your wonderful deeds of long ago.
> They are constantly in my thoughts.
> I cannot stop thinking about your mighty works.
> (Psalm 77:11-12, NLT)

God's work in our lives can be anything.

For me it's when I remember walking through past valleys, for example reflecting about how we got through Mum's cancer treatment, or when our much beloved dog suddenly passed away; those times that were really hard and we felt our strength was weak. When I look back, I can see the evidence of His grace and help, even in those moments when I couldn't tell Him the kind of help I needed or necessarily even feel Him working.

I can remember the joy of climbing Pen y Fan mountain in South Wales (the highest mountain in the south of Britain) in 2017. The physical challenge of walking up a mountain was in its own way like facing a giant. More than that was knowing as I climbed that I had looked up at the mountain in 2005 from the Brecon Beacon visitor centre and thought I'd never be able to do such a thing because of my physical health. When I reflect on those memories, I remember all God's interventions that helped me get to that point.

Reflecting gives hope, and hope, trust. God has helped us with the giants of our lives before, the visible and the invisible, and He can and will do it again.

It didn't take long for giants to appear after the flood, whether this was in actions, emotions or persons. Wherever our giants come from – ourselves, others, circumstances or the enemy – whatever the shape, size or form they take, and whenever they pop up in our lives, we can stand strong. Though we may feel like the size of a grasshopper compared to the challenge they represent, we can overpower them through our faith and trust. Though we find no sword or spear to hand, we can pick up a stone. Though our flesh feels weak or wants to tell us what to do, we take our giant-fighting strategy and strength from the Lord.

Precious women:

> Stand fast in *[your]* faith, be brave, be strong…
> Trust in *[firmly believe in the steadfastness, sincerity and capability of God] and* rely confidently *[don't be shaken or question, be secure]* on the LORD with all your heart
> And do not rely on your own insight *or* understanding.
> (1 Corinthians 16:13, NKJV; Proverbs 3:5)[72]

> *Father, thank You for the reassurance I see in Your Word about Noah not being perfect, or his family. You know I'm going to face challenges and situations that I won't know how to handle. But thank You that You have already conquered the giants. I don't want to be afraid of the giants in my life, now or when they arise. I don't want to rely on my feelings about how to fight them. I choose, Father, to trust in You. Thank You that You're lovingly working on me, carefully shaping and moulding me with Your 'potter's hand'.[73] Thank You for everything You've already done in my life. Help me to continue to remember, and I look forward expectantly to all that You're still going to do.*
> *Amen.*

---

[72] Author's additions in italicised square brackets.
[73] Jeremiah 18:6.

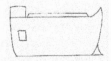

Chapter contemplations

- Think about your reactions to emotional giants that appear in your life and how you respond. Do you have a trigger for them to appear? Do you rush into the action they provoke?

- Reflect on those times that have felt like giants. How did the Lord help you through the circumstances, or to overcome them? Make some notes in your journal to help you remember what He did – whether these were things you didn't pick up on at the time, or the obvious triumphs.

- Make a colourful note for yourself using the Scripture verses above (1 Corinthians 16:13, NKJV; Proverbs 3:5). Stick it on the fridge or somewhere you'll see it every day to remind yourself to think about it.

Journal pages

12
As in the Days of Noah

The days of Noah and his family were many centuries ago. As we've explored their journey, we've understood their story has relevance and meaning to our lives today. We've gone beyond the familiar narrative of the animals going into the ark and considered how the family must have felt being aboard for more than a year; what they went through before, during and after the flood.

Noah was 950 years old when he died. He lived another 350 years after leaving the ark (Genesis 9:28-29). Noah would have witnessed generations of children spreading out like the vines he tended: fruitful and multiplying.

We can only imagine how Emzara, Tia, Sarah and Mert's stories ended. The only women to remember the evilness of the days before the flood; the sight as Noah hammered the planks into place; the feeling of the first raindrop; the experience of caring for the animals, living and supporting each other on the ark; witnessing the rainbow's first appearance, God's covenant banner; the new taste of meat; and the delight of children and grandchildren. The planning, the organising, the thinking, the everyday; the uncertainty they lived through, and the important role they played.

Humanity's self-will

As we learned when Ham shamed his father in the tent, the post-flood earth wasn't idyllic. Sin hadn't been swallowed up in the floodwaters. Families grew and the population continued to increase. Rather than following the principles God established when Noah and his family left the ark, unfortunately humanity's self-will dominated.

Even in those days, people were self-centred because they didn't spread themselves out and fill the earth, as God had said (Genesis 9:1), instead they preferred to gather together in a kingdom, which Nimrod, Ham's grandson, had established. They built the city of Babel; just like before the flood, the post-flood earth wasn't short on cities (Genesis 10:9-12; 11:4). The population was fully aware of what God had said – remember this is only two generations from Noah – yet they congregated towards this area and wanted to build a tower that would reach the sky. They were able to start because they had the architectural ability to build this kind of vast structure, to make bricks and bond them together. However, they didn't want to make a sky-high tower for no reason. They wanted to be famous, so it would stop them from being scattered over the earth (Genesis 11:4).

The consequence wasn't that they achieved their goal. Instead, the Lord saw what was happening, that the world was rapidly descending back to the pre-flood ways. So He

> confused the language of the entire earth; and from that place the LORD scattered *and* dispersed them over the surface of all the earth.
> (Genesis 11:9)

Though they weren't successful in their own effort, since that time we've continued to see the evidence of humanity's self-will. The urges of the world to create a global, worldwide perspective is strident. The need for itself to be glorified. The pull to live by the flesh. Each generation may have felt it was living in difficult days, but it feels like our days are even harder.

Difficult days

We could say that we're living in difficult days. We are witnessing many signs around us, and just because we're in these times, it doesn't make it easy. Paul spoke about what we're experiencing in 2 Timothy 3:1 where he said, 'In the last days dangerous times [of great stress and trouble] will come [difficult days that will be hard to bear].' We can agree. Life doesn't get easier, our days can be a struggle, and the unexpected shock of the pandemic made it even harder across the world, with the far-reaching impact it had and is still having. The world has experienced and continues to experience fear, uncertainty, financial hardship and loss of loved ones.

Within these 'difficult days', we're told about the change in people's behaviour too. *The Message* translation of what Paul says describes it well:

> Don't be naive. There are difficult times ahead. As the end approaches, people are going to be self-absorbed, money-hungry, self-promoting, stuck-up, profane, contemptuous of parents, crude, coarse, dog-eat-dog, unbending, slanderers, impulsively wild, savage, cynical, treacherous, ruthless, bloated windbags, addicted to lust, and allergic to God.
> (2 Timothy 3:1-4)

In this Bible version, we can see the repetition about 'difficult times' but there's also an instruction for us not to be ignorant. This all points towards us being able to recognise we're 'in the last days'. And when we read these verses, can't we see the evidence first-hand? People do behave in this way. It's important for us to be aware that despite any efforts of society, or form of control, it's not going to get any better. People are going to behave more and more in the manner we don't expect.

They will be headstrong in their determination. Remember the attitude at the Tower of Babel, where the post-flood earth looked towards itself, thinking they could be greater than God.

We're not able to live in a bubble away from everything. These days are difficult to bear because we can see it; we can witness what's happening. We will get stressed and shaken by events. We could get overtaken by worry. But as the world focuses more on its own strength, we have another perspective. We have hope: the unshakeable hope we have in God. We have faith: the same belief and conviction in what the Lord said that kept Noah building the ark despite the scepticism. We have confidence: the rainbow reminds us of God's faithfulness, when we see the arc in the sky.

It's only going to be holding fast to Jesus that will get us through the unfamiliar, the unthinkable and the unexplainable of these days.

The lens we look through

As believers, we have a choice about how we view the times we live in. We can pick up a pair of the earth's glasses and let everything we're told, think, speak, read, listen to or watch be taken as fact through the lens of the world's perspective. We can keep our minds fixed on worldly things (Colossians 3:2). We may even do this inadvertently because we've become used to relying on the information we take from the world's sources. Are we of this world? Is that what we signed up for when we gave our lives to Jesus? I don't think so.

As believers we are different because 'our citizenship is in heaven' (Philippians 3:20). Though my passport may state my nationality, my residence here is temporary:

> This means that anyone who belongs to Christ has become a new person. The old life is gone; a new life has begun!
> (2 Corinthians 5:17, NLT)

This spiritual awakening of new life gives us a new perspective. But it doesn't mean we won't be distracted with assessing worldly problems through its lens. This causes confusion. We can find our actions split. We can easily be led astray and find ourselves caught up in fighting the battles the world wants us to fight; to be emotionally affected through the messages promoted through various channels. Our vision and thinking about what's biblical can be dialled down because we're only focused on the literal.

The only way we're going to understand the times we're living in is to realise their context within the Word of God. We need to be vigilant. You see, our relationship with the Lord gives us a pair of heavenly branded spiritual glasses. We need to arm ourselves with them so that during these days we can 'resist the enemy in the time of evil' (Ephesians 6:13, NLT). We need to view what's going on in the world through the lens of living in the Spirit.

This is what enables us to be discerning, and not to be unwittingly deceived by Satan. He is a skilled expert at many forms of deception (John 8:44). These are 'difficult days' because of the schemes and strategies the enemy brings. We don't want to be blinded by them. We want to be able to rely on the Lord so 'we are not ignorant of his [Satan's] schemes' (2 Corinthians 2:11, addition mine). What could we be discerning about?

It might be anything – from the opinion of a friend, a speech by a politician, a social media post, an article, someone we admire, movies, the news, to a comment from someone we thought was a Christian. They can be things that are easy to believe in the moment, or that we can absorb without really thinking deeper about their meaning because we take what's being said as fact. We don't doubt it.

If we do this, we may find ourselves reacting either emotionally or choosing to take a certain action, without actually realising that we're being deceived. That's when we go into the territory of our reactions not coming from a stable biblical perspective. Perhaps unintentionally we find ourselves being led by the world's way of thinking. We find ourselves consuming its truth when it is only the Bible's truth we can rely on.

The Bible is the measure we need to use. This is what we need to return to and what we must use to check everything against. But remember, Satan will endeavour to draw us away from this. He wants us to be caught up in worldly things, in his deceptions. Let's not allow ourselves to be distracted. Let's keep wearing that spiritual lens, seeking His Word, because the truth sets us free (John 8:32).

Worldly things

For the time being we're living here, so it's not surprising that we're going to be confronted with worldly things. We can love living in the world, but we're not in love with it. We know God is a jealous God (Exodus 34:14). God doesn't want us to worship anything else but Him. We can't be in love with both God and the world. We can't serve the Lord if we're also serving the worldly desires of our flesh. We can't be so gullible as to what the world says that we're easily deceived:

> Don't love the world's ways. Don't love the world's goods. Love of the world squeezes out love for the Father. Practically everything that goes on in the world – wanting your own way, wanting everything for yourself, wanting to appear important – has nothing to do with the Father. It just isolates you from him. The world and all its wanting, wanting, wanting is on the way out – but whoever does what God wants is set for eternity.
> (1 John 2:15-17, *The Message*)

No matter how much money we have, no matter how many treasures or art collections we've stored, no matter how much we try to solve all the climate change problems, it doesn't have any everlasting substance. We need our treasures to be in heaven (Matthew 6:20). Why? Because there is an expiry date on this earth, it is going to 'pass away' (Matthew 24:35). But it's only going to pass away when God says it's time:

> Then I saw a new heaven and a new earth; for the first heaven and the first earth had passed away (vanished), and there is no longer any sea.
> (Revelation 21:1)

This doesn't mean, though, that we can't live our lives. After all, Jesus came so we 'may have and enjoy life, and have it in abundance [to the full, till it overflows]' (John 10:10). He wants us to enjoy our time here, to enjoy our lives 'to the full'. Jesus doesn't want us holed up in a cave waiting for Him. He doesn't want us to be afraid of making a mistake. We're not going to get it right all the time – we will mess up; we're not perfect, yet! But we need to be spiritually self-aware.

The difference is that we don't live the temporal abundant life. My life's purpose doesn't come solely through earthly pleasures, or the pursuits of earthly accolades. None of these things will remain when the earth passes away, so expending my energy in pursuing them doesn't bear any meaningful fruit. That's why our certainty and hope come from knowing Jesus and the knowledge that our lives go beyond the finite. Our bodies may fade, but we have eternal life through our belief in Him. As we live our lives in that awareness, we live not only abundantly but also with the understanding that we're living beyond what this world offers. The world isn't our home.

A thought on plant-based food

You'll remember from Chapter Ten, I spoke about how God introduced a new relationship with food. After Noah and his family left the ark, they no longer had to eat a vegan, plant-based diet, which the world had eaten since Adam and Eve. Now they could eat meat and every living thing. Wait a moment! Don't the words 'vegan' and 'plant-based' sound familiar?

Isn't it interesting that we're seeing an increase of veganism around the world? The number of vegans in Great Britain has risen four-fold in the last five years.[74] There are more plant-based foods available in the shops. More dairy-free milks for your coffee. It is referred to as the vegan era.[75]

I realise I've subconsciously taken this message on board and have started to eat less meat. I appreciate many of you reading this will follow different food diets for various reasons. I'm not saying what foods are good or bad to eat. I'm not saying if you're a vegan it means you're wrong. I'm not saying if you choose to cook more chickpeas, that you *shouldn't*. What I am saying is that through the discernment of the spiritual lens, we've got this worldly promotion about a particular type of diet.

Why use the word 'plant-based'?

This chimes with how the enemy spoke to Jesus in the wilderness when he quoted Scripture to Him and tried to twist its meaning (Matthew 4). Satan knows the Bible too. God speaks about giving 'every green plant for food' (Genesis 1:30). God was the first one to use this *plant food* type of language, yet after the flood God didn't say just to eat plant-based foods.

So, I wonder why the world is keen to embrace the kind of food eaten before the flood. Is it perhaps because we're living as in the days of Noah?

Living as in the days of Noah

We know the ark story isn't confined to the Old Testament. We've read other Bible passages where it refers to the flood.[76] Besides what we've already learned through following the story,

---

[74] 'Statistics', The Vegan Society, www.vegansociety.com/news/media/statistics (accessed 6th November 2020).

[75] Maja Talevska, 'The Age of Veganism: Vegan Health Statistics for 2020', *Veg World Magazine*, vegworldmag.com/the-age-of-veganism-vegan-health-statistics-for-2020/ (accessed 6th November 2020).

[76] Such as Hebrews 11:7; 2 Peter 2:5.

there is other relevance for our lives today. Though when I say about living in the days of Noah, I'm not talking literally, but that there is a comparison. And Jesus Himself made the deliberate choice to compare the last days to those at the time before the flood.

On the Mount of Olives, the disciples asked Jesus, 'When will this [destruction of the temple] take place, and what will be the sign of Your coming, and of the end (completion, consummation) of the age?' (Matthew 24:3). Jesus replied with many examples, and within this chapter there are many layers to the different times Jesus was referring to.

I believe that when Jesus talked about 'the days of Noah', this was in reference to the end of the Church age (Matthew 24:37). Why do I say that? Because Jesus was painting a picture here, drawing our attention to this particular Bible period. So why did Jesus talk about Noah?

State of the world

We've thought already about the world's behaviour before and during those ark-building days. The pre-flood earth was an evil and lawless place; though the flood was a shock to Noah, the state of the world wasn't. The state of our present-day earth has that similar feeling; nothing feels normal, we crave to return to what we had before, but when we think of those pre-pandemic days, was life really normal then? Though our lives might have felt like it, the world was already chaotic and unstable.

The word 'lawlessness' has become a familiar word, and not just because we know it from our Bible, but because the world uses it too. Lawlessness is around us more and more and there are many examples from across countries where journalists use the word 'lawless' or 'lawlessness' to report on the degradation of society.[77] Lawlessness 'is already at work' within the world (2 Thessalonians 2:7), and irrespective of any measures the world

---

[77] For example, Sean O'Neill, Fariha Karim, 'Public fear streets are lawless, say police chiefs', *The Times*, 5th July 2019, www.thetimes.co.uk/article/public-fear-streets-are-lawless-say-police-chiefs-pvzxq9g2j (accessed 6th November 2020).

takes, lawlessness is only going to increase, just like it did before the flood. That's one of the things I think Jesus is telling us to expect.

We know we're living in 'difficult days' now. We see the signs in many guises. There is so much pain and suffering throughout the world because of the escalation of darkness: genocide, persecution, modern-day slavery, people trafficking, corruptions, criminal activity, addictions, abuse, rioting and even more. Good is being called evil and what is evil is now being called good (Isaiah 5:20) – this is all about the switch in society, with less substance being placed on biblical principles and often going against them – an ever-increasing advancement of Satan's lies being listened to rather than God's truth.

We may be shocked at how rapidly things are changing in the world. We may feel like the minority, as Noah might have, within the majority. We may feel overwhelmed because we can see what's coming.

Something's impending

Noah knew from God that the flood was coming; it was an impending judgement. Meanwhile, the world was absorbed in its activities and its pleasures. Noah didn't throw a party when God told him everyone was going to die except for his family. I believe he preached even more earnestly (2 Peter 2:5), but no one listened.

The ark-building days were a visible warning sign of the flood. We have many signs around us of the clock ticking its countdown towards *something impending*. Jesus tells us that in these days:

> you will hear of wars and rumors of wars. See that you are not troubled; for all *these things* must come to pass, but the end is not yet. For nation will rise against nation, and kingdom against kingdom. And there will be famines, pestilences, and earthquakes in various places. All these *are* the beginning of sorrows.
> (Matthew 24:6-8, NKJV)

These signs are 'the beginning' of the end, not the end itself. So, if some of these are what we need to look out for, then are they on the increase or decrease?

Like Noah, we know what has been foretold and what's going to happen. So when Jesus is giving us an indication of what the last days will be like, He isn't doing it for no reason. He's telling us about what to expect: lawlessness, 'wars and rumors of wars', 'famines, pestilences, and earthquakes', so we won't be surprised, we won't try to understand what's going on through a worldly interpretation, but we'll understand spiritually about the times we're living in through the Word of God, and look to Him.

Where is this all leading, you might ask?

It's leading to another end. God didn't leave the Bible unfinished; there is a beginning and an end to its story. God told us what will happen – and remember, He didn't package it to flatter us; He tells the truth because that is who He is (Numbers 23:19). This time the *something impending* isn't another global flood, but the Tribulation.

The Tribulation is a specified judgement period including: the lawless one (antichrist) being revealed; wars; natural disasters; the holy Temple being rebuilt in Jerusalem, Israel, and then desecrated by the antichrist, and the world fully drawn into Satan's deception (2 Thessalonians 2:8-9; Revelation 6; Mark 13:14). The seven years of the Tribulation (Daniel 9:27) will end with the Second Coming of Jesus (Revelation 19:11) and the start of the millennial kingdom before the final judgement (Revelation 20:4-15).

That's a lot to take in, I hear you say. It is, and it also may not feel like the easy parts of the story. We may not like the thought of judgement, and it feels uncomfortable to think people will have to go through this.

Understanding what the Bible says about the last days and end times of the Tribulation is important, and we can read more in Revelation 6–19 and in other prophecies, such as in Ezekiel 38 and Daniel 12. Prophecies have already been fulfilled, such as Jesus' birth in Bethlehem[78] and the establishment of Israel as a nation in 1948,[79] and they will continue to be realised. Remember, all these prophecies have been given to aid our understanding through those spiritual lenses; they help us to perceive the *something impending* and this knowledge gives us hope, because despite what's going on in the world around us, we know our 'redemption is drawing near' (Luke 21:28).

Suddenly

Another comparison with the Noah story is the seven-day warning God gave to Noah about the rain. Though God told Noah the number of days, he never knew what time the rain would start falling on the earth – only God knew this time.

Jesus has given us warnings about what to look out for 'in the last days' as the world draws closer to entering into the Tribulation. But He hasn't told us *when* the Tribulation will happen. I can't give you the answer, neither can anyone else, because I believe it is a time 'Only the Father knows' (Mark 13:32, NLT). So what *suddenly* will start this season?

> The Arrival of the Son of Man will take place in times like Noah's. Before the great flood everyone was carrying on as usual, having a good time right up to the day Noah boarded the ark. They knew nothing – until the flood hit and swept everything away.
> (Matthew 24:37-39, *The Message*)

The arrival here isn't the Second Coming of Jesus back to the earth, which will happen at the end of the Tribulation (Revelation 19:11-16), but the rapture of His Church away from the world.[80] Why do I say this? Because I think that during the

---

[78] Jesus' birth was foretold by the prophet Micah (Micah 5:2).

[79] This prophecy was given to the prophet Ezekiel (Ezekiel 36:8-12; 37).

[80] Thomas D Ice, 'Are We Living in the Last Days?', see subheading, 'Last Days Vocabulary', paragraph 2, May 2009, Liberty University, digitalcommons.liberty.edu/cgi/viewcontent.cgi?article=1060&context=pretrib _arch (accessed 6th November 2020).

Tribulation people won't be able to have a 'good time'; life on the earth then will be even more disrupted because of the events that will take place during this period. So just like the rain *suddenly* fell on the pre-flood earth, believers will be *suddenly* taken beforehand:

> we who are alive and remain [on the earth] will *simultaneously* be caught up (raptured) together with them [the resurrected ones] in the clouds to meet the Lord in the air.
> (1 Thessalonians 4:17)

The rapture will be as unexpected to the world as the first raindrop which fell.

The time warning gave Noah an expectancy; even though he knew on day three it wasn't going to rain until day seven, it doesn't mean that he wouldn't have looked up at the sky to check. Like Noah, we don't know the hour, minute or second of the rapture *suddenly*, but we know that the day is coming closer from the signs Scripture gives us. So we need to be expectant:

> So you, too, must keep watch! For you don't know what day your Lord is coming. Understand this: If a homeowner knew exactly when a burglar was coming, he would keep watch and not permit his house to be broken into. You also must be ready all the time, for the Son of Man will come when least expected.
> (Matthew 24:42-44, NLT)

What does this expectancy give us? Understanding about the rapture gives us 'comfort' and encouragement because when it happens 'we will always be with the Lord' (1 Thessalonians 4:17). We will be removed from our temporary home to our eternal one.

I realise talking about the rapture may sound incredulous to anyone who doesn't yet believe. Perhaps as incredulous as a flood sounded back in the days of Noah?

I believe this is what the Word of God says. I believe this is the promise God gives to His children.[81] And for believers, it is the faith we have in the unseen things (Hebrews 11:1). But in our state of expectancy we don't wait around staring up at the sky, we continue to go 'about [our] Father's business' (Luke 2:49, NKJV, addition mine); we continue to live through 'difficult days' in the love and peace only Jesus brings; and we especially continue to make a difference and share the good news of His grace.

The difference

This is another time of God's great patience. But this time God isn't waiting for Noah to build the ark before He sends His judgement. No, God is waiting now so as many people as possible can be saved.

This is the difference in these days because we have a Saviour. We don't need to build an ark this time because our hope is in Jesus. Jesus is the ark. He's the only salvation for the world, and everyone can enter. This isn't an elite club. There isn't a limit on the number of places available:

> God sent his Son into the world not to judge the world,
> but to save the world through him.
> (John 3:17, NLT)

It isn't just Noah this time, it is the body of the Church across the world that has been given the saving knowledge of the gospel of grace (Romans 10:4), and as people search for

---

[81] I appreciate within the Church there are differing views about end-time prophecy. I am not claiming to be an eschatologist, neither that my thinking is the sole interpretation – this is my standpoint based on my Bible study. If this section raises questions for you, then I'd suggest returning to the Scriptures, asking Jesus for insight to understand His revelation (Revelation 1:1).

meaning, to find the truth they may look to us. But they'll need to see a difference.

Being different doesn't mean we won't experience emotions or feelings. It doesn't mean that we're not immune from everything that happens in life. We can't force ourselves to be different, or try to control our behaviour. It's not contrived. Our faith centres on relationship, not religion. Remember the Lord viewed Noah with 'favor *and* grace' because he walked with Him, and so do we (Genesis 6:8).

Walking with Jesus

Our relationship with Jesus is what we need to be developing, especially in these times. Jesus who calls us sister and friend (Mark 3:35; John 15:15). He doesn't sit on some high platform we need to visit to speak to Him. We don't need to do anything special to communicate with Him. Jesus has no expectations of us, all His heart's desire is that we simply walk with Him.

So often I see how the Lord cares about the little things, and it's having the daily walk with Him that makes it so much fun. It's an adventure being with the Lord. As Paul says about walking habitually with the Holy Spirit, 'seek Him and be responsive to His guidance' (Galatians 5:16). We may pray, 'Lord, find me a parking space,' but you know, He does care about them! I don't mean this trivially, but I have had experiences where I know the Lord has helped me with the little things of life.

Recently, I had a birthday gift idea for a friend I didn't feel entirely comfortable about. I think the Lord was nudging my spirit to say, 'Have you really thought about this?' but I pressed ahead and placed the order. The company emailed me back a couple of days later and said everything was out of stock. I said to the Lord, 'I'm sorry, I didn't listen. Where should I go?' He led me to another website and actually the items there were even better than my original idea. There were no ordering problems and the gifts were delivered in time. The Lord knew which presents were going to touch the heart of the recipient, and thankfully He got me out of the mess of following my own thinking.

You may be saying, 'Why does God care about presents or parking spaces?' But He does. He cares about us, about everything in our lives. He's the God who knows how many hairs there are on our heads (Luke 12:7). He's the One who formed those unique whorls of our fingerprints, in the womb (Psalm 139:13). He wants to be part of all of our lives.

So why doesn't He answer the big questions we may have? That's one question I'd love to know the answer to! I'm still waiting on Him for some of those 'big question' answers, like what to do next. Ultimately, it all comes down to trusting Him, like they had to on the ark. They had to wait after the rain stopped; it wasn't safe for them to leave because of the floodwaters.

We can't know everything. We're not God. But we can learn to hear His voice (John 10:27), and that starts with talking to Him. No grand words needed, no lengthy prayers, just start with a simple 'Jesus'.

I found I was talking with Him even more during the pandemic. It was the only way to get through what was going on, living in a constant state of flux. And more than ever, don't we need Jesus' peace to guide our decisions?

Just like I found with the present shopping, we can think we know best. We so need His wisdom in our lives. If we don't feel at peace to go somewhere or to do something, we need to listen to Him.

We shouldn't feel embarrassed or foolish for talking to Jesus daily. Yes, there are times when we pray or come together to bring specific issues to the Lord, to gather with fellow believers to encourage and be encouraged, to be taught, to worship, to support and love each other, but we can't solely rely on this.

We don't want to stop ourselves from experiencing the joy, adventure and peace that come from letting Jesus into every aspect of our lives. We don't want our relationship with the

Holy Spirit to be like a window we open but only get a glimpse through before we shut it again. Keep the window open.

We can not know, but still go

I think we'll find the levels of uncertainty will escalate as the fallout of the pandemic continues around the world. Whether we return to what we once called 'normal' or there's a new norm, living in these Noah-like days means we're going to experience even more strangeness, even more things happening in the world.

The women of the flood faced many different types of unknowns. What about our unknowns? And how do we know what to do in them?

You still may face questions about where to go next in your life, or what to do about your particular situation. I've learned through the story of the ark that I can't fathom it all out. The most important thing to realise is that there is movement, there is progress, even while we are waiting. We can *not* know, but still go through uncertain times. God hasn't forgotten us.

Just as Emzara, Tia, Sarah and Mert had to manage and collect provisions, just as Noah built the ark, they progressed with *what they knew*. They didn't stop caring for the animals during all the months of waiting while the ark was afloat, and they could have felt discouraged at the lack of any signs.

It doesn't mean they wouldn't have liked to know, that Emzara wouldn't have loved Noah to answer all her questions. And it's OK for us to feel like this, to want answers; for us to ask the Lord, 'What shall I do?' – though we need to remind ourselves when God doesn't immediately answer, He's still working. I hold on to Proverbs 20:24: 'The LORD directs our steps, so why try to understand everything along the way?' (NLT).

I don't need to understand everything. Once I start worrying, thinking about *pleasing people,* the *shoulds,* or making those comparisons about *the view of what I do,* that's when I can get embroiled in trying to make sense of it all and try to take control.

That's when I walk through every day feeling afraid rather than at peace.

Other times we have a sense of direction, to take a step forward. Again it's OK to not know everything but still make the move; trusting as your foot lifts that you 'will hear a word behind you, "This is the way, walk in it," whenever you turn to the right or to the left' (Isaiah 30:21).

When we sense God's voice in our spirit calling us to walk forward when we can only see the edge of the next paving slab on the path, we can confidently step out. We're not going to necessarily have God tell us to build an ark in regard to every unknown!

Sometimes we are going to have to trust, have faith and make that movement. And it's at that point we'll have a sense of peace about the turn we've started to make. How are we going to know it's His peace unless we have the relationship with Him first? Our friends may all be saying one thing, but we need to know in our spirit that the choice of step to go right or left comes from Him. Because once we start to walk in that way, there will be more unknowns. It's about learning to be led by Him and, crucially, giving Him the control in our life for Him to lead because He wants to guide us (Psalm 48:14).

We'll all face different shapes of unknowns: we can be daunted by taking the next tiny step; we can make ourselves scared by their size and the various kinds of giants they attract; we can be distracted from our daily victories, whatever their proportion; but we mustn't be disheartened or discouraged. We need to reassure ourselves with the remembrance of past times, but also by the realisation that what we're doing right now is progress. It's about the everyday, consistent walk with Jesus. Looking to Him, listening to His wisdom and being obedient.

Surely our heart's desire is to be obedient? So if we're being obedient to what we're doing today, if we're alert to His 'still small voice' (1 Kings 19:12, NKJV), if we feel His peace, then we need to continue to trust in Him.

The core companions we need to live in these times are a personal relationship with Jesus and obedience. They have a key role in how we'll show Jesus to the world around us – how we'll be able to tell the good news of a Saviour who doesn't just have only eight places on His ark.

Showing Jesus in our lives

We may not all feel like great evangelists. We may struggle and think we're not good enough, that our lives aren't all together, but that's why we're here. That's what Jesus tells us:

> Let me tell you why you are here. *You're here to be salt-seasoning* that brings out the God-flavors of this earth. If you lose your saltiness, how will people taste godliness? You've lost your usefulness and will end up in the garbage.
>
> Here's another way to put it: *You're here to be light*, bringing out the God-colors in the world. God is not a secret to be kept. We're going public with this, as public as a city on a hill. If I make you light-bearers, you don't think I'm going to hide you under a bucket, do you? I'm putting you on a light stand. Now that I've put you there on a hilltop, on a light stand – shine! Keep open house; be generous with your lives. By opening up to others, you'll prompt people to open up with God, this generous Father in heaven.
>
> (Matthew 5:13-16, *The Message*, italics mine)

If you eat food without any salt, the meal doesn't taste right, but when you add salt, it draws out the blend of flavours. Each of us brings our unique seasoning, the gifts that God has given us (Romans 12:6-8) to the world. We're godly salt. We're the salt the earth needs. Not all of us will stand on a platform and preach, but actually what's more important is what we show in our lives. It's the significance in what we may perceive as insignificant that makes the difference.

You see, it's all about not doing things for the wrong reason. The world needs kindness; it soaks it up like a sponge. But there's a difference between worldly kindness and God-centred kindness. We don't let good ideas motivate us; we let God-ideas drive what we do. We want to shake our God-given 'salt-seasoning' so others can taste His goodness. We want them to know about His love for them, because we know He loved us first (1 John 4:19). And it's our love for Him, the personal relationship we have, that enables us to scatter the significance of small things as we go through our daily lives. What do I mean?

It's about *showing* Jesus at every opportunity. Letting our 'character' and 'conduct' shine out against the behaviour of the world (1 Peter 1:15). Walking with Jesus and being 'led by the Spirit' brings sensitivity to what we do (Romans 8:14).

The small things all bear a witness. How we treat people, what we say and how we act. We won't necessarily see the bigger picture about what God is doing in others' lives through how we show Him. Our act of love and obedience to what God tells us to do may not always lead to an immediate reward. We don't sit like dogs obeying a command, expecting a biscuit. But if we feel God say to do something, then let's obey. It's like the time I went shopping and I felt the Lord say to me to buy a pint of skimmed milk. I had no idea why; I didn't need it, but I bought it anyway. I then stopped by to see a friend. They mentioned they needed milk and that particular amount. Ah, so that explained why I had the pint in my shopping!

It's about showing God's love in all manner of ways, even if it doesn't make sense. But we also need to tell people about God's love too.

Telling people about Jesus

Though the last days are difficult and the darkness intense, we can't be afraid to shine. The world needs Jesus' light and that's why He tells us to display it. Difficult times mean there will be difficult decisions, where we will be the only light in a dark room. Shining results in attention being drawn to ourselves, but while we're here we need to be bold, to not be afraid to stand out.

We're not 'ashamed of the gospel' (Romans 1:16). People more than ever need to know about Jesus. We know there is more to life than living here. We can't hide our faith because we want to please people, because we want to be accepted.

Noah didn't just tell people, 'I'm building a big boat because I feel like it.' No, he told them the truth. He was a 'righteous man' (Genesis 6:9). We can't be complacent and live our lives like the people did during the days of Noah, 'eating and drinking' (Matthew 24:38), enjoying temporary worldly pleasures. There is an urgency to these times. We don't know when we'll be 'caught up … in the clouds' (1 Thessalonians 4:17), but until that unknown time, we need to be bold and courageous. We need to season the earth, and shine.

Our lives as believers don't need to be all together to share about Jesus. It's the glory of what the Lord has done and is continuing to do in our lives that bears a witness. The difference for us is, even among struggles and 'difficult days', we have the Lord.

Everyone in the world has their individual unknowns, like us, but *we have the certainty of knowing where we'll go*. Jesus told us what these times would be like – we know that what's going to happen in this world isn't going to make sense unless we have assurance in Him. But we remain hopeful in His hope, keeping our eyes fixed 'on the things above' (Colossians 3:2) through our spiritual lens. Don't we want others to experience our certainty too? For them to know beyond doubt 'the peace … which transcends all understanding' (Philippians 4:7)?

We're here for these times

The women of the ark all had a role in the time they were born into. We have been born into these times. We are here on purpose. We weren't randomly allocated to our birthday. God knew us before we were formed (Jeremiah 1:5).

We're not accidents. We're not unwanted. We're chosen women. We're women living in the world now, 'for such a time as this' (Esther 4:14).

We don't need to be *there* to serve the Lord. We're *here* in this community, this country, this continent. So scatter the unique kind of salt you bring into the place where you are. Radiate His light into the surrounding darkness. Don't measure your actions or yourself against the enemy's lies or what the world says.

We may remain nameless like Mrs Noah, but it doesn't devalue *who we are*. What we might think of as small – a smile for someone serving us in a store, a conversation with a stranger, washing our neighbour's car, a gift for a friend, a word of encouragement, or saying to someone we'll pray for them – if they're done out of our heart's desire of obedience and relationship with Jesus, then they are not random. They are from Him:

> So, as God's own chosen people, who are holy [set apart, sanctified for His purpose] and well-beloved [by God Himself], put on a heart of compassion, kindness, humility, gentleness, and patience [which has the power to endure whatever injustice or unpleasantness comes, with good temper].
> (Colossians 3:12)

You are cherished. You are loved. You are a daughter of the most High God. It's time to step out and shine.[82]

Father, living in these 'difficult days' gives me so many different emotions. The world is incredibly crazy with so many things happening that don't always make sense, but You know all things,[83] You alone are God. Thank You that Your Word helps me to recognise the particular times I'm living in.

---

[82] Isaiah 60:1
[83] Psalm 139:4.

Help me to discern the signs and to be comforted by Your promises. Holy Spirit, I so want You to lead me. Refresh me again and enable me to know when You're directing me so I can be sensitive to You. I want to serve You, Jesus, in these days, to show and tell people about the hope found in You. Remind me not to be caught up with how the world and the enemy want to deceive me with their agenda. And that even as I pray this, I may not know everything, but I can confidently trust in You and wait, being certain that I am moving forward; knowing that as I take the next step You will guide me. Just like the women of the flood, I can not know, but still go. Keep in my heart all that You've wanted me to understand from this book. I pray that I can encourage others from all that I've learned. All praise to You, Jesus.
Amen.

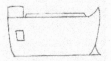

Chapter contemplations

- Reflect on whether you get caught up in understanding things through worldly ways. Pray and ask the Lord for spiritual discernment. Practise the habit of questioning what you're listening to against whether it's biblical. Be brave and make godly choices not to fill your mind with the things of this world.

- Ask the Holy Spirit daily how you can show and tell of Jesus in the big and little things of your everyday. Read Galatians 5:16.

- Spend some time with your journal and the Lord thinking about everything He's revealed to you as you've read. Make notes, particularly about any areas you need Jesus' help with, or what you sense in your spirit. Remember to come back to them again in the future so you can encourage yourself with what the Lord has done.

Journal pages

Last Word

If you've read this book and you've never given your life to Jesus before, then 'now *is* the ... time; ... now *is* the day of salvation' (2 Corinthians 6:2, NKJV). God is patiently waiting, you've not left it too late. All you need to do is believe and give your life to Him by praying the prayer below.

> *Father, thank You so much for giving us Your Son, Jesus. I believe Jesus died on the cross and He took all my sins; His blood washes me clean. I believe Jesus rose again on the third day, and He is alive today. I'm righteous in Your sight. I'm chosen and precious and part of Your family. Thank You, Father, for this new amazing and eternal life I have in You – for Your unconditional love. In Jesus' name, Amen.*

Welcome! This is the start of an incredible time for you, as you get to know your Father more and more and listen to His heart for you. If you don't have a Bible, then either purchase one or download a free Bible app, and start reading.

There's no routine to being a believer. God loves to spend time with us. He loves us wanting to get to know Him. Reach out to a Bible-believing, Spirit-filled church in your area[84] so you can get to know other believers. There are great Bible-based

---

[84] If you're in the UK then this is a UK Church directory you could use: www.findachurch.co.uk (accessed 27th November 2020). Otherwise try searching online for churches close to you.

teachers out there and lots of online resources.[85] Build up your faith and strengthen your spiritual muscle. I pray for blessings in your life and, above all, that in these days you'll be filled with overwhelming peace and follow His lead.

---

[85] Some of these include Christian broadcasters so you can watch, listen and access other helpful materials, such as from: Premier, www.premier.org.uk (accessed 27th November 2020), Trinity Broadcasting Network, www.tbn.org (accessed 27th November 2020) and United Christian Broadcasters, www.ucb.co.uk (accessed 27th November 2020).
Behold Israel will help you to understand more about Israel and its importance within Bible prophecy, beholdisrael.org (accessed 27th November 2020).

Acknowledgements

I always read the acknowledgements; as a writer I'm intrigued to read about what other writers have said and the process they've been through to have a book published.

Hopefully this won't sound like one of those long 'thank you' speeches at an award ceremony, but having now been through the book-writing process, it makes me understand why it matters so much and why you want to show your appreciation.

I know the best 'Author'[86] around and He has been so brilliant throughout this experience. Thank You, Jesus, for Your grace which has inspired, energised and empowered me (1 Corinthians 12:6). Thank You for everything You've done and will continue to do in my life.

Thank you for reading these pages and also the book! I hope you haven't just enjoyed reading it, but that it has spoken to you too. I know I will be returning to what the Lord has helped me understand many times again. Please do get in touch with me – you can find me on social media; I'd welcome your feedback. I also think books are like cake; you want others to savour a slice, so please recommend or leave a review.

I can't list everyone, or we really would be here beyond the space allowed, so if you know me, then I include you in this journey:

---

[86] Hebrews 12:2.

- Mum – what a wise, faithful daughter of God you are. I'm so thankful for you.

- Thank you to *all* my friends and family for their encouragement and belief in me. A shout-out to: Grandma Margaret, Berrin, Steph, Karen, Nigel, Dr Charlotte and Louis, Jayne, Sue and Gary, Leigh-Anne and Suman.

- Thank you, Richard Buxton, for your encouragement back in those MA days when you told me to keep writing the Noah stories. Thank you to all my fantastic fellow MA writers and the English and Creative Writing Department at the University of Chichester.

- Thank you *team NKBSG* – once you go from being an aspiring author to an actual one you realise how much writing a book is a team effort. Aunt Carolyn, you got to read a very early, very different-looking draft of this book; thank you for getting the vision. Jemma Smith (like Berrin, you've told me many times to get writing, and look, I did!), Vivien, Liz, Audrey, Donna Kirstein, you've all given your time and input into this book. Thank you for your care and honest insight. Within this group are crucially: Nicki, Sheila and the amazing team at Instant Apostle who have supported the book, guided me, answered my many questions and sharpened my writing skills!

  Now to Him who is able to [carry out His purpose and] do superabundantly more than all that we dare ask or think [infinitely beyond our greatest prayers, hopes, or dreams], according to His power that is at work within us, to Him be the glory in the church and in Christ Jesus throughout all generations forever and ever. Amen.
  (Ephesians 3:20-21)